Challenging Environmental Mythology:
Wrestling Zeus

Jack Dini

Foreword by Dr. Jay Lehr

SCITECH
PUBLISHING, INC.

ISBN: 1-891121-29-4

Published in the United States by
SciTech Publishing, Inc.
5601 N. Hawthorne Way
Raleigh, NC 27613

Distributed to the trade by
William Andrew Publishing
13 Eaton Avenue
Norwich, NY 13815

Cover illustration and design by Suzanne K. Beckley
Typesetting by Keith M. Stein

Manufactured in the United States of America

Cataloging-in-Publications Data applied for

Printed on acid-free paper

10 9 8 7 6 5 4 3 2 1

Books are available in quantity for promotional or premium use. Write to Director of Marketing, William Andrew Publishing, 13 Eaton Avenue, Norwich, NY 13815. For information on discounts and terms call (607) 337-5000.

Library of Congress Cataloging-in-Publication Data

Dini, J.W.
    Challenging environmental mythology: wrestling Zeus / Jack W. Dini ; foreword by Jay Lehr.
        p. cm.
    Includes bibliographic references and index.
    ISBN 1-891121-29-4
        1.   Environmentalism. 2. Environmentalism-United States. I. Title

GE195.D36 2003
363.7-dc22

2003017918

Acknowledgments

I would like to thank a number of people who helped me bring this book to fruition. Dr. Jay Lehr's book Rational Readings on Environmental Concerns (Van Nostrand Reinhold, 1992) provided the initial inspiration for me to start accumulating the information contained in this book. I am indebted to Jay (and his wife Janet) for their help along the way and also for Jay's generous commentary on the book. Dr. J. Gordon Edwards of San Jose State provided helpful discussions and support and so did Dr. Hugh Elsseasser of Lawrence Livermore National Laboratory.

I owe a special debt of gratitude to Sylvia Baxley Heidemann of the American Electroplaters & Surface Finishers Society (AESF) for suggesting that I write a column for Plating & Surface Finishing (P&SF) the technical journal of the AESF. The column served as basis for the book and continues to be the main vehicle prompting me to learn more about environmental issues. Thanks are also due to Don Berry, editor of P&SF for his help and patience.

The editors at SciTech Publishing, Merrill Douglas and Brent Beckley, opened a whole new world of writing for me. Even though I had published extensively (many technical articles and a book), I had much to learn about wordsmithing and their talents were always evident. Particular thanks to Brent for his final editing and support which made me want to include him as co-author.

Lastly, my thanks to my wife Anne for her support. She is my best and favorite critic and though we don't always agree on all issues discussed in the book her input has always been most helpful.

Preface

I am a supporter of the original intention of the environmental movement. I love animals, scenic parks, and think that clean air and water are critically important. Contained within the pages of this book, however, is a fundamental criticism of the environmental movement in its current state. The forward thinking scientists who looked at the problems of our environment and lobbied for change are heroes in their own right. However, their desire to learn, educate, and affect public policy has turned into a movement of mythological proportions. This movement has become a culture of scare tactics, junk science, and politicking in order to attain their goals. Anyone criticizing this is literally locked in battle with the denizens of Mount Olympus (hence the subtitle Wrestling Zeus).

My guess is that most readers will find the information contained within this book to be news. In other words, "that's news to me!" The environmental movement, using a supportive (and forgetful) media to its greatest advantage, has never acknowledged the myriad of positive changes that have occurred over the last few decades. The truth is not being told, or is hidden in obscure places where few tread. The media, which is biased in many cases and scientifically challenged in others, continues to abide by the premise of "bad news is good news," allowing the environmental movement to tighten its chokehold on our knowledge of critical issues. John F. Kennedy once told a Yale audience that the greatest enemy of truth was not the lie but the "persistent, persuasive, unrealistic myth." On a daily basis, we hear unrealistic myths about our environment.

This book is an attempt to provide you with the other side of the story.

As an engineer in the electroplating area, I spent years researching and working with the Environmental Protection Agency regarding pollution prevention. During my tenure with the Lawrence Livermore National Laboratory, I was the Waste Minimization Coordinator for the Materials Fabrication Division. It was in this capacity that I began my research into environmental issues and have read over 3,000 scientific and popular articles and over 500 books. As my research continued, I became very aware of unreasonable regulations and money wasted on efforts based on opinion and politics instead of sceintific fact.

To address these issues, I have been writing a column on environmental issues for over five years. Like Melvin Benarde in his book, *You've Been Had*, what I have found in my literature review is a chasm between the facts in the scientific and medical community on environmental issues, versus what is being presented in popular periodicals, on television, radio, and in books.

I realize that many will not like what I have to say in the following chapters. However, I make no statements without a solid scientific basis. In other words, I am not standing on a soap box, but on what I believe to be a concrete foundation of scientific consensus on each of the issues presented.

My sincerest hope is that this book will live up to its moniker as a true challenge to environmental mythology and that readers will come away from it with a sounder knowledge of what science is really saying.

Let's climb the steps of Olympus together, and wrestle with Zeus for a bit.

Foreword

Over the past three decades the United States and many of its global partners have wrought the most successful grass roots effort to improve and preserve our environment, which had fallen into disrepair after the second World War and the subsequent industrial revolution. We began as a nation divided among those who were part of the problem and those who were part of the solution. However, by the end of the first decade of effort, nearly all Americans as well as citizens of most of the developed world could count themselves as environmentalists - all of them working hard to protect and improve the quality of our air, water, and soil.

Although the job is not now and never will be complete, the gains we have made as a population pulling together are truly amazing. We should take the time to celebrate our significant achievements. The environmental principles that are a part of conducting our lives and doing business have become more and more clear to corporations, municipalities, and individual citizens, all of whom are adopting a new sense of environmental responsibility. This is evident in new products and manufacturing processes, local government affairs and the attitudes of most American families.

Industry today tries to find ways to cut down on waste, save energy, and make their products more environmentally attractive. They look for cooperation with traditional adversaries, such as the government and environmental advocacy groups, in order to achieve win-win alliances.

But for some environmental activists, environment preservation and cleanup efforts appear never to be satisfactory. Environmental issues become a vehicle for achieving unrelated and unidentified ideological or economic goals. The American who would once proudly claim to be an environmentalist and support efforts to curb dumping of raw sewage into rivers and lakes soon became entangled by association in deviant efforts to remove minuscule levels of alleged toxins from some waters - even though there was no evidence that the chemicals in question posed either ecological or public health threats.

Under a new environmental banner, more radical environmentalists redefined pollution and contamination using increasingly lower measurements; as low as a part per trillion, which is the same ratio as one second in 32 years. Often the mere ability to detect the presence of a chemical sufficed to fit this new-fangled definition of pollution.

Everyone reading these words knows these things to be true and evident. Most of us wring our hands in frustration. Few of us do any thing substantial to counteract it. Most of us do not have the capacity to effectively debate our adversaries. Jack Dini has given us the tools to fight misinformation whether it be malicious or honestly attained.

In Challenging Environmental Mythology: Wrestling Zeus, Dini analyzes the foundation of every major environmental issue now clouded with political rhetoric. At a time when the public can be thoroughly confused between fact and fiction regarding our environmental concerns, Dini comes along to unravel our problems with the surgical precision of a brilliant physicist and the unusual ability to communicate with simple jargon free language that we can all understand.

His brief essays deal with poorly understood distortions of human risk from the countless headlines which strike fear into the hearts and minds of our friends and neighbors daily; often causing them to take arms against a paper tiger. When you reach the end of this book you will be enriched by wonderful science you will have learned from this modern Mr. Wizard and elated by the lifting of the weight of pessimism from your shoulders.

Dr. Jay H. Lehr
Science Director, The Heartland Institute

Permission to Publish

Everything presented in this book is updated and expanded material which originally appeared elsewhere. Except for two chapters, all of the information is from a column I write for Plating & Surface Finishing (P&SF). The two chapters ("Poopophobia" and "The EPA's Fat Chance,") that did not appear in P&SF originally saw publication in the Journal of Irreproducible Results (JIR). A number of chapters also appeared in the Standard Handbook of Environmental Science, Health, and Technology, edited by Jay H. Lehr and Janet K. Lehr and published by McGraw-Hill in 2000. They include: "Indoor Air Pollution - Is Your Home Sick?," "DDT: The Real Story," "The Single Molecule Theory of Chemical Contamination," "Hormesis: Mother Know's Best," "Nature: Frail or Force to be Reckoned With?," "Killer Rocks - Please Spend My Money Here!," "One in a Million - Human Health Risk," "Radiation - It's What You Think You Know," "Radiation Hormesis - A Little Bit Means A Lot," "Poverty is the Worst Carcinogen," "Environmental Indicators - Gimme the Bad News, Doc!," "Bad News is Big News," and "Environmental Education - Breeding Brainwashed Activists?"

Permission to publish this information has been granted by The American Electroplaters & Surface Finishers Society, McGraw-Hill, and the Journal of Irreproducible Results. I gratefully thank them for permission to use the original work as a basis for the information in this manuscript.

Jack Dini
September, 2003

Contents

Section I:

Pollution

Chapter 1

Can Someone Please Define Pollution?

Pollution is a difficult word to define. Entire books have been written on the subject without presenting a valid definition. One example is *Industrial Pollution: Poisoning Our Planet* by Eve and Albert Stwertka.[1] In spite of their rhetoric on dirty skies and murky rivers caused by industry, I could find no true definition of pollution.

This is not unusual. The word "pollutant" is left undefined, but is used to condemn the substance to which it refers. As with "flower" and "weed," the eye of the beholder determines the essential definition of "pollution."[2] My dictionary says: To pollute is to make physically impure or unclean: to contaminate especially with man-made waste." This is at best, underdefining the word.

To better define pollution, we must answer some questions. How much waste or contamination can be considered pollution? To what level does a substance's presence within an environment make it a pollutant?

The concept of pollution includes two parameters: dirtiness and danger. We spend money to reduce pollution to reach the other pole: cleanliness and safety. Max Singer notes, "While safety is often talked about as an absolute requirement, modern science can detect such infinitesimally small "dangers" that the decision about how much "health threatening" pollution to allow becomes a matter of preference or efficiency, not an absolute."[3] In other words, the equipment we use to find "pollutants" in an environment is capable of finding the most minuscule trace of a substance. Our concerns are with tiny amounts of substances whose degree of harm is extremely difficult to prove. Past examples include Alar on apples, crabmeat from Canada, and anchovies from California. If you wait another week or two, you'll find some other scare on TV or in the local paper.

Hugh Ellsaesser says, "Nothing has polluted the objectivity of science like the semantic monstrosity into which the word pollution has been converted. It now conveys only two attributes – something that defiles or degrades and is also of anthropogenic origin. That is, natural pollution is an oxymoron. If you recognize a pine grove, a row of eucalyptus, or an orange grove by their fragrance, you are detecting pollution. You are detecting plant-emitted hydrocarbons, which are even more reactive than auto exhaust in the photochemical process that generates Los Angeles smog. However, in today's sea of political correctness, you call it pollution only at peril to yourself."[4]

Julian Simon suggests that we classify pollution as either *aesthetic* or *health related*.[5] Aesthetic pollution is the hardest to define, as it is subjective in nature. For instance, the noise of children at play can be delightful to one person, while another considers it a nuisance, or "noise pollution." Another example is the rows of turbines that make up a wind farm. We have thousands of these turbines in the hills surrounding my hometown of Livermore, California. I think these are beautiful structures reminiscent of the work by the artist Christos. My wife thinks they are hideous. Another example of aesthetic pollution can be summed up in one word. Perfume.

Health related pollution is easier to measure. The simplest and most accurate measure of health is length of life, summed up as the *average life expectancy*. After thousands of years of almost no improvement, in the past 200 years developed countries have seen a long upward climb in life expectancy. In the United States life expectancy was 45 years in 1800; today it is 79 years for women and 73 for men. "Poor countries have gained a 15 or even 20 year increase in life expectancy since the 1950s."[5] All this gives no ground for increased alarm about pollution. If pollution is increasing, and reduces life, why are we getting older? If anything, the increased life expectancy supports the general assessment that pollution has been decreasing.

Factors other than reduced pollution such as improved nutrition, and medical advances have also contributed to greater life expectancy. But it is important to note that the decline of the old pollution-caused diseases accounts for much of the increased longevity. For those of us in developed countries, the great killer disease pollutions of the past (cholera, typhoid, diptheria, etc.) have been conquered. These days the majority of people die of diseases of old age, such as heart disease, cancer, and strokes. And, as Simon points out: "There seems to be no evidence that the increase in cancer is due to environmental carcinogens; rather it is an inevitable consequence of people living to older, more cancer prone ages."[5] Stephen Fried, in his book *Bitter Pills* quotes Dr. Albert Kligman: "In the first two decades I practiced, we were heroes. We were stopping polio and syphilis, conquering acute infectious disease. Now everything has changed. We have an older population. People don't die of polio and meningitis; they now live long enough to get cancer and hypertension and depression and any number of day-to-day troublesome things. Despite all our technology, despite all our stuff, people don't like us — because we are dealing with chronic conditions for which we don't have immediate and long-term treatments."[6]

Many people have tried to push for a return to our hypothetical pristine past. They dream of returning to a paradisiacal time or place — Eden, Arcadia, the Golden Age that they have never known, but are sure once existed. A time and place without the pollutions of irresponsible industry. In fact, such paradises never existed. Folks commonly look back to a certain phase of a nation's history that they consider ideal but they tend to ignore the seamy side of that era. As Evan Eisenberg notes, "They conveniently forget about the drafty houses where a glass of beer could freeze in your hand while you stood with your back to the fire, or streets laden with horse manure, flies and the smell of urine filling the air, spreading disease and irritating the lungs."[7]

One last thing I will mention here, parts of which are covered in later chapters in more detail. Countries undergo environmental transition as they become wealthier and eventually start getting cleaner. The reasons for this are complex, but the wealthier a nation is the more it values and the more it can afford to pay for a healthier environment and environmental amenities. A corollary to this is that environmental organizations from developed countries worry more about pollution, forest loss, and species diversity rather than human health in poor countries.[8] Often this results in devastating effects on the local populations, and the overall health of the people living in the Third World.

Here are some examples;

- A decision by officials in Peru, based on studies from the United States EPA that stated chlorine may create a *slight* cancer risk, led them to stop chlorinating much of the country's drinking water. This has been blamed for a devastating cholera epidemic in which 700,000 illnesses were recorded, as well as 6,000 deaths in Peru and other countries in Central and South America in the early 1990s.[9]

- Malaria, which was being controlled by DDT, has proliferated since the West pressured other world governments to ban its use. Malaria has returned in frightening numbers, killing millions annually in the Third World. Western priorities were imposed on people who may have made a different trade-off had the choice been solely theirs.[10] (See Section 2: Chapter 8 - DDT: The Real Story)

- A book edited by Melissa Leach and Robin Mearns of the University of Sussex documents how the myths of deforestation and population pressure have damaged parts of the Sahel region of the Sahara desert. Westerners have forced inappropriate measures on puzzled local inhabitants in order to meet environmental activists' preconceived notions of environmental change.[11]

Pollution remains underdefined, and it seems that finding an all encompassing definition is like trying to catch the pot of gold at the end of the rainbow. Rhetoric filled texts about dirty skies and water continue to fuel a firestorm of debate over a subject that has no real definition. If pollution causes premature death, then it makes sense that our recently newfound longevity contradicts the belief that we are dirtier and more dangerous than ever before. And, as detailed later, our beliefs about pollution are often inappropriately imposed on other nations resulting in catastrophic health crises.

References

1. Eve Stwertka and Albert Stwertka, *Industrial Pollution: Poisoning Our Planet*, (New York, Franklin Watts, 1981)

2. Hugh W. Ellsaesser, "Air Pollution: A Different View," *Water, Air, and Soil Pollution*, 11, (1979), 115

3. Max Singer, "Alternative Perspectives on the Earth's Prospects," in *Global 2000 Revisited*, ed. H.W. Ellsaesser, (New York, Paragon House, 1992), 53

4. Hugh W. Ellsaesser, "The Ozone Layer" in *Standard Handbook of Environmental Science, Health, and Technology*, eds. Jay H. Lehr and Janet K. Lehr, (New York, McGraw-Hill, 2000), 20.29

5. Julian L. Simon, *The Ultimate Resource 2*, (Princeton, New Jersey, Princeton University Press, 1996), 92

6. Stephen Fried, *Bitter Pills*, (New York, Bantam Books, 1998), 295

7. Evan Eisenberg, *The Ecology of Eden*, (New York, A.A. Knopf, 1998), 164

8. Gregg Easterbrook, *A Moment on Earth*, (New York, Viking, 1995), 331

9. Christopher Anderson, "Cholera epidemic traced to risk miscalculation," *Nature*, 354, (November 28, 1991), 255

10. Lorraine Mooney, "The WHO's Misplaced Priorities," *Wall Street Journal Europe* (August 25, 1997)

11. Melissa Leach and Robin Mearns, eds, *The Lie of the Land*, London, The International African Institute, (1996), 2

Chapter 2

The Good Old Days...Weren't

"We have wished, we ecofreaks, for a disaster or for a social change to come and bomb us into the stone age, where we might live like Indians in our valley, with our localism, our appropriate technology, our gardens, our homemade religion guilt free at last!" — Stewart Brand in the *Whole Earth Catalog*[1]

This statement references the psychological propensity of environmentalists to return to the "good old days," a pristine age when humans lived in harmony with the earth, never polluting, always taking only what they needed.

Before we delve into the myriad of difficulties of living in the past, let's take a look at why people hold such a strong belief in the "good old days." David Hume, the Scottish philosopher, said, "The humor of blaming the present and admiring the past is strongly rooted in human nature, and has an influence even on persons endued with the profoundest judgment and most extensive learning.[2] Daniel Lazare states that when confronted with the problems of the modern world, the first instinct of religious societies is to retreat to some long lost Eden where everything was good, clean, and honest.[3] Since some have accused environmentalism of being a religion, Lazare's comments can be tied with the desire to return to the past.

"In a strange way it can be comforting to suppose, as does current environmental doctrine, that until recently everything was fine but now the world is falling apart. The sentiment that until recently everything was fine grants high standing to nostalgia, one of the strongest human emotions, while the idea that everything is suddenly falling apart is among the oldest of human sentiments. Women and men who lived in every age seemed to believe that they just missed being born into a better time and instead were cursed to exist among unprecedented tumult."[4]

Fact is, the good old days weren't really that good. Let's start with the "outdoors" environment and then discuss the "indoors" environment as well.

Let's go way back, to what could be considered the most pristine environment, the neolithic age. As P.J. O'Rourke points out, "Neolithic man was not known for leaving his camp site cleaner than he found it. Ancient humans blighted half the earth with the indiscriminate use of fire for slash and burn agriculture and hunting drives. They caused desertification through overgrazing and woodcutting in North Africa, the Middle East and China. And they were responsible for the extinction of mammoths, mastodons, cave bears, giant sloths, New World camels and horses and thousands of other species."[5]

A bit farther up the timeline is ancient Greece or Rome. Even these great ancient cities faced pollution issues. Plato was already discussing deforestation problems, while other writers complained of problems in the atmosphere and the urban environment. Solon, in the sixth century B.C., ruled that blacksmith activities should be transferred outside the city of Athens in order to avoid noise and pollution. Vitruvius (75-26 B.C.) described city climates and climactic conditions in the Roman cities and the allusion on smoke pollution also appears in the poems of Horace (85-68 B.C.) [6]

A study of crusts formed on stone monuments in Arles and Bologna in the periods 1180-1636 and 1530-1887 respectively provided evidence of past air pollution. Chemicals found in these crusts were also encountered in the smoke from experimental wood fires. This approach confirms the presence of air polluted by wood combustion in the towns of southern France and northern Italy during the Middle Ages up to the Pre-Industrial Age.[7]

Let's go forward in time now to the New World before Columbus made his trip. William Denevan of the University of Wisconsin, a leading authority on the Americas before the whites, debunks what he call the "pristine myth" of pre-Colombian North America. He reports that by 1492 Indian activity throughout the Americas had modi-

fied forest extent and composition while expanding and creating grasslands. Denevan also states that in addition to burning forests to create prairies, Indian action before 1492 caused many woodlands to convert from mixed tree species to single species dominant stands.[8] In more recent years, we hear a lot about the inhabitants of the rainforest. Tom Sterling, a Briton who concerns himself with the Food & Agriculture Organization of the United Nations, says the following to illustrate how critically we must read reports on the rainforest and its inhabitants. "The assertions of romantically disposed outsiders that all Indians live in perfect harmony with themselves and nature and consider only whites to be the enemy is utter nonsense."[9] Some environmentalists consider these tiny communities as a model for society. They wish to spend their lives in small economies, living under government imposed self sufficiency, and not relying on the world over the horizon for any important goods or services.[10] For example, Rudolf Bahro, a founding member of Germany's Green Party has said that "people should live in socialist communities of no more than 3,000, consuming what they produce and not trading outside the community."[11] However, as shown by Michael Crichton in his book, *Travels*, most people who live in tiny, self sufficient communities do so in abject misery.[12]

Now let's move up the timeline from the end of the Civil War to the early 1900s. Otto Bettman reports, "This period of history leaves many with an image of an ebullient, carefree America with the fun and charm of the Gilded age and the Gay Nineties. The gaiety was only a brittle veneer that covered widespread turmoil and suffering. The good old days were good but for the privileged few. For the farmer, the laborer, the average breadwinner, life was an unremitting hardship."[13] A variety of pollutants made life in industrial cities unhealthy and degrading. Untreated smoke belched constantly from factory smokestacks. Streets were caked with animal wastes and the oozings of clogged sewers and littered with the overflow of uncollected garbage piled on the sidewalks.

Today many decry the automobile as a culprit of our nostalgic desire to return to cleaner days. But they have forgotten the pollution caused by the modes of transportation that cars replaced. Joseph Bast quotes Fred L. Smith, a former senior policy analyst for the EPA and now president of the Competitive Enterprise Institute, who gives this vivid and unpleasant description of the impact horses had on American cities less than 100 years ago.

"Cars create pollution. But it is also true that cars may well have dramatically reduced overall pollution. A horse produces approximately 45 pounds of manure each day. Flies, dried dung dust, and the smell of urine filled the air, spreading disease and irritating the lungs. On rainy days, one walked through puddles of liquid waste. Occupational diseases in horse related industries were common."[14]

Again from Bast, "Smith goes on to report that New York City in the 1890s had to dispose of 15,000 dead horses every year, a huge public health and environmental problem. Often these rotting corpses were hauled in open air wagons to the edge of town where they were dumped into huge kettles and heated over coal fires (without emission controls) until they were reduced into grease, later to be sold to the manufacturers of candles and lubricants. The remains of the dead animals that could not be sold were dumped, untreated, into the nearest river or lake."[14] It was no different in other parts of the world. Analysts in Victorian London might confidently have predicted that if the city kept growing at 19th century rates, all the streets would be a foot deep in horse manure by the 1950s.[15]

Edward Tenner notes that "New York City's horses alone produced over 300 million pounds of manure annually. In high density urban environments, massive tonnages accumulated, requiring constant collection and disposal."[16] I would also like to note here that the horse drawn carriage was the most dangerous vehicle ever driven in the United States.[17]

To complete our vision of the good old days outdoors, the "simpler way of life" has an appeal for many, but they do not see the surprisingly high costs associated with their desire. One student of Julian Simon calculated that if farmers in the United States used 1918 agricultural technology instead of modern technology, forswearing tractors and fertilizers in order to save natural resources, "we would need 61 million horses and mules and it would take 180 million acres of cropland to feed these animals or about one half the cropland now in production. We would need 26-27 million additional agricultural workers to achieve 1976 production levels with 1918 technology."[18]

So, let's go indoors now to see just how good the old days were. You are probably familiar with historic sites that feature reconstructed houses from earlier times, such as Colonial Williamsburg in Virginia. A small village of this sort has been constructed at the Historical-Archaeological Experimental Center in Lejre, Denmark. It comprises of four dwellings and eight workshops and outhouses from the Danish Iron Age. In the paper from Henrik Skov et al, we will see the reports of a pilot study that measured the indoor concentrations of NO_2 (nitrogen dioxide) and benzene and the personal exposure of a woman living in one of the reconstructed houses.[19] These chemicals were tested because they are known emissions from the combustion of wood, which would have been used for heating and cooking. As the authors state; "NO_2 is known not only to irritate the respiratory system resulting in coughing, but also to lead to chronic lung diseases, etc. Benzene is known as a strong carcinogenic compound leading to leukemia."[19]

The woman in the test stayed mostly indoors, (which was historically accurate) spending only one to two hours outside each day – about six percent of her time. One week's average NO_2 levels in micrograms per cubic meter in the reconstructed house provided the following results: personal exposure 61.6, outdoors 9.9 (a distance about 20 meters from the house), at the fireplace 107.4 and at the bed 110.8. These values are at least 200 percent higher than on today's busy roads. The concentration of benzene in the house (45.8 micrograms per cubic meter) was about five times higher than on a busy road in Copenhagen and more than twice as high as the concentrations faced by people living and working in Copenhagen. The conclusion from the pilot study is that people in the Iron Age were exposed to levels of indoor air pollution that must have affected their general health to a greater degree than today.

Another way to be exposed to the "good old days" indoors today is to visit a Third World country. The Danish house in the study provides only 1/3 the exposure of a typical woman living in rural areas in the Third World today.[20] Several World Health Organization (WHO) studies have shown that average daily indoor air pollution in developing countries is 1,000 to 2,000 percent or more above the recommended maximum threshold.[21] An estimated 2.8 million people die annually because of indoor air pollution worldwide, mainly because of the burning of solid fuels (e.g. coal, wood and dung) for heating and cooking in the home in developing countries.[22]

The next time you think about or hear someone talk or write about how wonderful it would be to live in some bygone era, remember that these times were far from idyllic. That past world was in no way spared the problems we consider horrendously our own, such as pollution, addiction, or urban blight. Although concern over pollution is greater today than at any time in the past, our external and internal environments are cleaner than they have been for many centuries. Our present days are far more healthier and cleaner than the "good old days."

References

1. Stewart Brand, quoted in Michael Fumento, *Science Under Siege*, (New York, William Morrow & Co., 1993), 335

2. David Hume, quoted in J.L. Simon, "Why do we hear prophecies of doom from every side?", *The Futurist*, (Jan/Feb 1995), 19

3. Daniel Lazare, *The Frozen Republic*, (New York, Harcourt Brace & Co., 1996), 2

4. Gregg Easterbrook, *A Moment on Earth*, (New York, Viking, 1995), 111

5. P.J. O'Rourke, *Parliament of Whores*, (New York, Atlantic Monthly Press, 1991), 199

6. K. Karatzas, "Preservation of Environmental Characteristics as Witnessed in Classic and Modern Literature," *The Science of the Total Environment*, 257, (2000), 213

7. P. Ausset, F. Bannery, M. Del Monte and R.A. Lefevre, "Recording of Pre-Industrial Atmospheric Environment by Ancient Crusts on Stone Monuments," *Atmospheric Environment*, 32, (1998), 2859

8. William Denevan, quoted in Easterbrook, (1995), 94

9. Tom Sterling, quoted in Thomas David, *Miracle Medicines of the Rainforest*, (Rochester, Vermont, Healing Arts Press, (1997), 64

10. Gregg Easterbrook, *A Moment on Earth*, (New York, Viking, 1995), 375

11. Rudolf Bahro, quoted in W.H. Baarschers, *Eco-Facts & Eco-Fiction*, (London, Routledge 1996), 3

12. M. Crichton, *Travels*, (New York, Alfred A. Knopf, 1988), 211

13. Otto L. Bettman, *The Good Old Days—They Were Terrible*, (New York, Random House, 1974), xi

14. Joseph L. Bast, Peter J. Hill and Richard C. Rue, *Eco-Sanity*, (Lanham, Maryland, Madison Books, 1994), 113

15. Peter Huber, *Hard Green*, (New York, Basic Books, 1999), 26

16. Edward Tenner, *Why Things Bite Back*, (New York, Alfred A. Knopf, 1996), 262

17. Melvin J. Grayson and Thomas R. Shepard, Jr., *The Disaster Lobby*, (Chicago, Follett, 1973), 153

18. Julian L. Simon, *The Ultimate Resource 2*, (Princeton, New Jersey, Princeton University Press 1992), 287

19. Henrik Skov et. al, "Exposure to Indoor Air Pollution in a Reconstructed House from the Danish Iron Age," *Atmospheric Environment*, 34, (2000), 3801

20. J. Zang and K.H. Smith, "Hydrocarbon Emissions and Health Risks from Cookstoves in Developing Countries," *Journal of Exposure Analysis Environmental Epidemiology*," 6 (1996), 147

21. Bjorn Lomborg, *The Skeptical Environmentalist*, (Cambridge, United Kingdom, Cambridge University Press, 2001), 182

22. *Rethinking Risk and the Precautionary Principle*, ed. Julian Morris, (Oxford, England, Butterworth Heinemann, 2000), 202

Chapter 3

Indoor Air Pollution – Is Your Home Sick?

You are a good person because you are energy conscious. The windows in your home are tripled paned. You insulated the attic and put new insulation and vapor barrier in your walls. You weather stripped every door. Your house is a model of energy efficiency. And it is making you sick.

We pay enormous amounts of time, energy, and expense regarding outdoor pollution and its health impact, but people **spend up to 90 percent of their time indoors**.[1] Indoor air is the most polluted atmosphere to which we are exposed. We inhale approximately 20,000 liters of air each day, 18,000 of which is indoors, making indoor air quality a critical issue.[2]

Starting in the 1970s energy consciousness convinced people to make our homes and public buildings more energy efficient. Home and office buildings were made more airtight so heat would not escape. And, while outdoor air regulations were being tightened, Federal ventilation standards were relaxed for public buildings and workplaces. Larry Laudan reports that "Energy saving measures recommended or mandated by the EPA and OSHA have reduced the number of air changes in a house or small office building from about four changes per hour to about one per day.[3] Basically, when we are indoors we are breathing the same air continuously, which increases our chances of inhaling toxins, allergens, and disease.

As Laudan writes in his book *Danger Ahead*, this is part of the reason why "air in airplanes and office buildings is now much staler than it used to be and why the frequency of 'sick buildings' seems to be on the rise. The clear trade-off is that as structures become more airtight, the risks of all those airborne diseases to which we are prone from the carcinogens in tobacco smoke and cooking oil, to the smoke from our wood stoves and the germs from our office mate with the flu go up in direct proportion to the extent that we are achieving energy savings as we seal

So what is the table showing us?

10 chemicals (out of the 20 tested for) were prevalent in the air samples. For New Jersey, an 11th chemical, carbon tetrachloride was present.

In New Jersey indoor air medians exceeded the outdoor air medians for every chemical in every season, usually two to five times. Similar results were observed for median indoor and outdoor concentrations in North Carolina and North Dakota.

Outdoor air was noticeably cleaner in North Dakota than in New Jersey or North Carolina.

In other words, indoor air in almost every case, was far more polluted than outdoor air in all three areas, even in New Jersey (the area with the highest incidence of industry). There are some other very interesting results from this study which are not seen in the table.

- Smokers had significantly elevated breath levels of benzene, styrene, ethylbenzene and m,p-xylene.
- Use of hot water in homes for activities such as washing clothing and dishes, and bathing or showering is the main source of airborne chloroform.
- Benzene exposure while filling gas tanks may exceed 1000 micrograms per cubic meter. People who reported filling their gas tanks had twice as much benzene on their breath as a person who did not.
- Moth crystals and room air deodorizers are responsible for noticeably increased concentrations of p-dichlorobenzene. About 80 percent of the homes in the survey had these materials.
- Tetrachloroethylene exposures are elevated by wearing and storing dry cleaned clothes.
- Activities identified with increased exposures included pumping gasoline, visiting service stations, visiting dry cleaners, traveling in a car, refinishing furniture, painting, building scale models, using pesticides, and smoking.

So, outside of the aforementioned study, what are the most common pollutants in our homes? You might be surprised at the variety of natural and man made chemicals inside a typical home, in addition to particulate material and potent allergens. Some of the more im-

up the places where we live and work."[4] It is estimated t
of new buildings display classic "sick building syndrome'

Several published studies have compared indoor air ar
exposures. A paper by Wallace et. al. summarized the res
study of the relationship between the concentration of a nt
lutants measured indoors, outdoors, and from a personal
each person carried during their normal daily activities.[6]
ies, known as the TEAM (total exposure assessment method
vincingly demonstrated that an individual exposure to cer
ants can be markedly higher than expected given the conc
those pollutants outside. Meaning, those pollutants are in

The objective of the study was to measure exposures to
organic compounds in the air inside the home, outdoor ai
water, and breath. We will focus on the indoor and outdoor
eters to stay on track. Three areas in the United States were
provide data – Bayonne/Elizabeth, New Jersey; Greensbo
Carolina; Devil's Lake, North Dakota). Bayonne/Elizabet
geted because of the high concentration of chemical and p
refining operations. Greensboro was chosen because it is
size to Bayonne/Elizabeth and it has small industries, but no
or refining operations. Devil's Lake was selected to provide d
population of a small agricultural town far from any industry.
for the study is shown in the table below for indoor and outd

Weighted medians for air samples (micrograms per cubic met

| Chemical | New Jersey | | Greensboro, NC | | Devil's L |
	Personal Air	Outdoor Air	Personal Air	Outdoor Air	Personal Air	C
1,1,1 Trichloroethane	17	4.6	32	66	2.5	
Benzene	16	7.2	9.8	0.4	---	
m,p-xylene	16	9.0	6.9	1.5	6.2	
Carbon tetrachloride	1.5	0.87	---	---	---	
Trichloroethylene	2.4	1.4	1.5	0.2	0.5	
Tetrachloroethylene	7.4	3.1	3.3	0.7	5.0	
Styrene	1.9	0.66	1.4	0.1	---	
p-dichlorobenzene	3.6	1.0	2.6	0.4	1.7	
Ethylbenzene	7.1	3.0	2.5	0.3	2.1	
O-xylene	5.4	3.0	3.6	0.6	2.7	
Chloroform	3.2	0.63	1.7	0.14	0.38	

(a) Lance A. Wallace, et. al., *Environmental Research*, 43, (1987), 290

portant ones include: tobacco smoke; carbon monoxide; radon; oxides of nitrogen (NOx); formaldehyde; volatile organic compounds (VOCs); chlorinated organic compounds; dust and particulates; house dust mite allergen; cat allergen; fungi and fungal spores; bacteria; pollen; and asbestos fibers.[1]

Your house is a polluted nightmare and you would be safer living on the street, right? Don't worry, the risk of illness from any one of these is small and most do not pose a serious threat to health. According to Paul Harrison, dust mites constitute one of the most important indoor problems because of the role they may play in the incidence and prevalence of asthma.[1]

Other pollutants may not pose as serious a threat as is believed. Everyone has heard the scare press about asbestos, and billions of dollars have been spent in removing it from buildings, even though it may actually pose a negligible threat. In her book *Haunted Housing*, Cassandra Chrones Moore writes: "As published research mounted during the 1980s, it became increasingly clear that asbestos levels in buildings, including schools, are barely detectable and over 1,000 times lower than levels found to be harmful. Richard Doll, who originally demonstrated that occupational exposure to asbestos increased lung cancer rates, stated that the risk to building occupants from exposure to asbestos was minimal, comparable to that associated with smoking a half a cigarette in a lifetime."[7] A Canadian government commission made the following statement: "Even a building whose air has a fiber level up to 10 times greater than that found in typical outdoor air would create a risk of fatality that was less than 1/50th the risk of having a fatal accident while driving to and from the building."[8]

Even though most of these pollutants pose little risk, there are many measures you can take to rid your home of some of the more serious ones. First, stop anyone from smoking in the house. There are over 2,000 compounds that have been identified in cigarette smoke, none of which you want in the air in your home. Next to tobacco smoke, carbon monoxide is the most obviously identifiable problem. Purchase some carbon monoxide detectors and place them next to potential sources of toxic fumes such as the furnace or hot water heater. If the detectors find serious levels, contact a professional to check the appliances. Another important step is to have a vacuum cleaner that "really vacuums." Rein Roos, in discussing the "clean air syndrome" refers to vacuum cleaners as dust recyclers.[9] Most vacuum cleaners simply pick dust up, throw it around the room in particles you can't see, which then coagulate and form particles you can see, that you try to vacuum up again. Make sure that your vacuum has a filter system which will not allow the dust particles to escape. Other strategies include a combination of improved ventilation, source removal or substitution, source modification, and air purification.

Findings from many studies have proven that the same air pollutants covered by federal regulation for outdoor air are usually found at much higher levels indoors. In our efforts to conserve energy, we have made our homes and office buildings "sick" which also increases our chances of being ill as well. However, it is not really necessary to call the EPA to your home and apply for Superfund cleanup. Most of the pollutants, even some that have been tagged as deadly by the media, do not pose a serious health threat, and simple changes in daily routine can make a great difference.

References

1.   Paul T.C. Harrison, "Health impacts of indoor air pollution," *Chemistry & Industry*, No. 17, (September 1, 1997), 677

2.   Nicholas Tate, *The Sick Building Syndrome*, (Far Hills, New Jersey, New Horizon Press, 1994), 28

3.   Larry Laudan, *Danger Ahead*, (New York, John Wiley & Sons, 1997), 158

4.   Larry Laudan, *Danger Ahead*, (New York, John Wiley & Sons, 1997), 35

5.   Nicholas Tate, *The Sick Building Syndrome*, viii

6.   Lance A. Wallace et. al., "The TEAM study: Personal exposures to toxic substances in air, drinking water, and breath of 400 residents of New Jersey, North Carolina, and North Dakota, *Environmental Research*, 43, (1987), 290

7.   Cassandra Chrones Moore, *Haunted Housing*, (Washington, D.C., Cato Institute, 1997), 159

8.   Nicolas S. Martin, "Environmental myths and hoaxes: The evidence of guilt is insufficient," *Vital Speeches*, Volume LVI, No. 14, (May 1, 1990), 434

9.   Rein A. Roos, *The Forgotten Pollution*, (Dordrecht, Holland, Kluwer Academic Publishers, 1996), 96

Chapter 4

Nitric Oxide — From Pollutant to Molecule of the Year

Nitric oxide (NO) is the simplest of the oxides of nitrogen. Other oxides of nitrogen include nitrous oxide (N_2O) and nitrogen dioxide (NO_2). Nitrous oxide, also known as laughing gas, is used as an anesthetic while nitrogen dioxide exists mainly as N_2O_4 and forms highly toxic brown fumes.[1] The focus of this chapter, nitric oxide is the gas found in cigarette smoke and smog. Nitrogen oxides are major components of air pollution from auto exhaust and industrial combustion. Ground level ozone is formed by a photochemical reaction of nitrogen dioxide to yield nitric oxide and an oxygen atom. The nitrogen oxides also contribute to the formation of acid rain.[2] Obviously, nitric oxide is part of a family of bad gases.

Or is it?

An industrial gas and environmental pollutant, nitric oxide was named "Molecule of the Year" by Science magazine in 1992. Editor Daniel E. Koshland, Jr. wrote: "In the atmosphere it is a noxious chemical, but in the body it is amazingly, under doses, is extraordinarily beneficial."[3] In 1998, the Nobel Prize for Medicine was awarded for discoveries concerning nitric oxide as a signaling molecule in the cardiovascular system. Tiny puffs of nitric oxide mediate an extraordinary range of biological properties in our bodies, ranging from destruction of tumor cells to the control of blood pressure.[4]

In the body, nitric oxide is extremely short-lived. It exists for about 6-10 seconds and then is converted by oxygen and water into nitrates and nitrites.[5] The amount of research concerning nitric oxide in the human body is staggering, and here are some of the observed effects of nitric oxide on physiological systems and diseases as listed by Anne Kuhlmann Taylor[2]:

- Lungs – Nitric oxide reduces blood pressure in the lungs without affecting the pressure in the rest of the body

- Heart – It has long been known that nitroglycerin (which chemically releases nitric oxide) can relax the blood vessels near the heart and increase blood flow. New drugs that also release nitric oxide are being developed.

- Shock – White blood cells release large amounts of nitric oxide to kill bacteria; however, this release can also cause blood vessels to dilate, leading to dangerously low blood pressure. Thus, nitric oxide has had both helpful and harmful roles in septic shock.

- Cancer – White blood cells may use nitric oxide they release to fight tumor formation.

- Brain – Nitric oxide mediates intercellular communication in the brain.

- Diagnostic analyses – Some inflammatory diseases can be diagnosed by analyzing nitric oxide production by the lungs and intestines.

- Impotence – Studies of the role of nitric oxide in penile erection led Pfizer to develop Viagra.

- Alzheimer's Disease – The role of nitric oxide produced by the body in neurodegenerative diseases is also being studied. Although some studies indicate a toxic effect, the evidence is not conclusive.

Other observations include:

- The disease schizophrenia involves a disturbance within the arginine-nitric oxide pathway in the brain.[1]

- A novel coating that emits nitric oxide may offer a new way to fend off microbial buildup on catheters, artificial hips, and replacement cardiac valves.[6]

- Increasing the concentration of nitric oxide in the lungs may represent a means of offsetting hypoxia, a deficiency in oxygen reaching the tissues of the body which is noted particulary at high elevations.[7]

- Some of the most dramatic potential applications of nitric oxide are in parasitology and tropical diseases.[4]

· Nitric oxide may help treat sickle cell anemia.[8]

Taylor also reports: "Nitric oxide is the first gas to be approved as a drug product. Although oxygen and nitrous oxide (laughing gas) have been used medically for many years, they never were subjected to the current rigorous approval process. Most of the anesthetic gases are actually volatile liquids; thus, nitric oxide is unique in the pharmaceutical industry."[2]

Not only is nitric oxide being used in the medical industry as a pharmaceutical, recent research indicates that nitric oxide concentration in the atmosphere changes noticeably before an earthquake, possibly opening the door to being able to predict these potentially deadly occurences.

Tokiyoshi Matsuda and Motoji Ikeya reported that the concentration of nitric oxide eight days before the Kobe, Japan earthquake was 199 ppb (parts per billion), about 10 times higher than the average peak of 19 ppb. The concentration of nitric oxide was also found to have increased before other major earthquakes with a magnitude greater than 5.0 in Japan. They state: "Atmospheric discharges by electric charges or electromagnetic waves before earthquakes may have generated the nitric oxide."[9] Also: "Emanation of nitric oxide from the ground might be expected before an earthquake if active oxygen (called peroxy radicals) were formed underground by the fracture of rock and reacted with nitrates in nature." However, any theory about nitric oxide and earthquakes must also take into account weather conditions and vehicular traffic. Studies have shown that nitric oxide is produced in high quantities as a result of intense heating and/or shock waves from a lightning strike.[10]

Also, nitric oxide is generated by fuel combustion, so the effects of human activities complicate the interpretation of the data. Matsuda and Ikeya suggest that nitric oxide should be measured at a remote area to study the background levels of nitric oxide there, so one can distinguish the concentration of nitric oxide produced in nature from that generated by human activities.[9]

Nitric oxide is also responsible for love in nature. Until recently neurobiologists have been unable to identify the missing link that triggers a firefly's burst of light. It appears that this phenomenon also depends on nitric oxide.[11] As mentioned earlier, it is also responsible for love in the human world as well, so fireflies and men have something in common.

As seen in the example of nitric oxide, time often passes and a "Pollutant of the Month" is upgraded to "Molecule of the Year." Next time you hear about a pollutant, remember that in 10-20 years scientists may discover how important this "pollutant" is for human existence. Carbon monoxide may be the next example because this deadly gas that kills thousands each year could improve transplant patients' chances of survival, or even help people with asthma breathe more easily.[12]

References

1.   Anthony R. Butler, "The biological roles of nitric oxide," *Chemistry & Industry*, (October 16, 1995), 828

2.   Anne Kuhlmann Taylor, "Nitric oxide - From pollutant to product," *Chemical Innovation*, 30, (April 2000), 41

3.   Daniel E. Koshland, Jr., "The Molecule of the Year," *Science*, 258, (December 18, 1992), 1861

4.   Carl Djerassi, *NO*, (New York, Penguin Books, 1998), 2

5.   Solomon H. Snyder and David S. Bredt, "Biological Roles of Nitric Oxide," *Scientific American*, 266, (May 1992), 68

6.   J. Gorman, "Materials use nitric oxide to kill bacteria," *Science News*, 160, (September 15, 2001), 165

7.   Cynthia M. Beall, et al, "Pulmonary nitric oxide in mountain dwellers," *Nature*, 414, (November 2001), 411

8.   Damaris Christensen, "Nitric oxide may help treat sickle cell anemia," *Science News*, 157, (January 29, 200), 78

9.   Tokiyoshi Matsuda and Motoji Ikeya, "Variation of nitric oxide concentration before the Kobe earthquake, Japan," *Atmospheric Environment*, 35, (2001), 3097

10. Edward Franzblau and Carl J. Popp, "Nitrogen oxides produced from lightning," *Journal of Geophysical Research*, 94, D8, 11,089 (August 20, 1989)

11. Elizabeth Pennisi, "NO Helps Make Fireflies Flash," *Science*, 292, (June 29, 2001), 2413

12. Liz Fletcher, "Life's a Gas," *New Scientist*, 172, (November 24, 2001), 39

Chapter 5

Global Warming: The Controversy Rages On

I guess the best way to describe the global warming controversy comes from a quote John Christy saw in the *Times* of London. "The science of 'climatology,' the *Times* notes, has become "calamitology.'"[1] The press and environmental groups continue to pound the public with calamitous news about global warming, rising sea levels, severe storms, glacier and polar ice melting and the potential health effects of climactic change. We have also heard many times of the reluctance of the current administration to sign the Kyoto Protocol, an environmental treaty intended to restrict the production of greenhouse gases and other pollutants in the century to come. Hopefully, by the end of this chapter, you will see that there is a lot of research showing that global warming may just not be as serious as we are led to believe and that many people are asking us to make extremely expensive conclusions from limited information.

During the past 100 years the earth has become warmer. The questions are: how much warmer, who is responsible, and is it really a disaster in the making?

Since 1900 the Earth has warmed by 0.5 degrees Celsius (0.9 Fahrenheit). Well, wait a minute! It seems to me that a less than 1 degree Fahrenheit rise in temperature in a century's time is not as serious as the doomsayers would have us believe. But, let's keep going and try to find someone to blame for the "warming."

Most folks attribute the rise in temperature to a 50% rise in carbon dioxide. However, here's an interesting fact about carbon dioxide. Most of the temperature rise occurred *prior to* 1940, but over 80% of the additional carbon dioxide entered the atmosphere *after* 1940.[2] How can increased greenhouse gases explain a temperature rise that occurred before the major increase of these gases in the atmosphere?

As the George C. Marshall Institute reports, "The climate record over the last 100 years provides no support for the idea that human activities, such as burning coal and oil for energy, caused the early 20th century global warming. Natural factors must have caused most of that warming."[2] The Marshall Institute also reports, "Water vapor and water in clouds absorb nearly 90% of the infrared radiation, while carbon dioxide, methane, and the other minor greenhouse gases together absorb little more than 10% of the infrared radiation. Therefore, most of the greenhouse effect is natural and caused by the different forms of water in the atmosphere."[3]

Robert Essenhigh, Professor of Energy Conservation at Ohio State University, believes that global warming is not the result of human activity but a natural occurrence within a 100,000 year planetary cycle. He states that scientists have vastly underestimated the significance of water in the atmosphere as a radiation absorbing gas, and that humans are responsible for less than 5% of atmospheric carbon dioxide. He does not believe this percentage can be driving the rise in temperature.[4] Essenhigh is not the only one to report this type of statistic. James P. Collman in his book *Naturally Dangerous* says that the share of carbon dioxide from human activities is less than 3% of the total, and this is the quantity that the Kyoto Protocol proposes to reduce or minimize.[5] C.R. de Freitas reports, "anthropogenic carbon dioxide emissions are only about 3% of the natural cycle and less than 1% of the atmospheric reservoir of carbon."[6]

Prior to 1979, there was no really accurate method to measure temperature around the world. Most readings were taken at land based locations, which created an interesting problem. Temperature measurements in urban areas were inherently faulty. As cities grew and expanded, urban temperature readings increased but rural readings did not. This is called the "heat island" effect. We all know that downtown is normally much warmer on a summer day than in the suburbs because of the heat absorption by streets and sidewalks. Robert C. Balling reports, "As cities grow, they inevitable get warmer, and thermometers in the urban environment will display a rise in temperature through time that could be mistaken for a greenhouse signal. Somewhere between 5 percent and 25 percent of the global warming of the past century is not real at all — it is a trend that comes from the urban data that contaminates the temperature record."[7] I guess not everyone knew that downtown is hotter.

In 1979 satellite temperature readings became available. Data from satellites, which have now been available for over 20 years, show that the temperature of the Earth has increased about 0.04 degree Celsius per decade, a rate similar to that for the previous 100 years. As Jay Lehr notes, "Critics have charged that they are not accurate but weather balloon observations correspond so closely to satellite readings that this argument has been discarded. The next criticism was that the satellite readings did not correct for orbital decay, but this was easily corrected and that argument has now been dropped."[8]

Some researchers say that the sun might be the reason for the increase. Jay Lehr and others note, "One natural factor in climate change may be variations in the brightness of the sun, over decades to centuries, that are in step with changes in the sun's magnetism, which has a period of roughly 11 years and is known as the sunspot cycle. Climate models suggest that changes of roughly 0.5% in the sun's brightness would produce global average temperature changes of about 0.5 degrees Celsius over a century or so." Lehr adds, "The almost perfect correlation between the sun's magnetic activity and the earth's temperature is too close to be readily dismissed."[8]

Why don't these low numbers get into the public realm so we can really discuss this issue? Especially the seemingly minuscule amount of actual "warming" or the fact that Mother Nature supplies between 95-98% of the carbon dioxide in the atmosphere. Seems to me like the so-called "innocent" is the culprit in this situation. However, if Mother Nature or the universe is to blame, can't we assume that it is meant to be this way and not to worry so much about it?

Let's take a look at a few of the doomsday scenarios that environmental groups tie directly to global warming in order to keep their agenda fresh in our minds.

Predictions from the Intergovernmental Panel on Climate Change (IPCC) in 1980 assumed that the polar ice sheets would melt, causing a catastrophic 25 foot rise in sea level, which certainly is an attention getter. Regarding this catastrophic assumption, here's one response. "The idea that global warming would melt the ice caps and flood coastal cities seems to be mere science fiction. A slight increase in temperature – whether natural or mankind induced – is not likely to lead to a massive melting of the ice caps, as sometimes claimed in the media. Also, sea-level rises over the centuries relate more to warmer and thus expanding oceans, not to melting ice caps.[9] Coupled with this, the IPCC keeps changing their estimates of sea level rise. As computer simulations have become more sophisticated, projections of rising sea levels have become much smaller. The 25 feet increase in 1980 fell to three feet by 1985 and then to one foot by 1995. Obviously, sea level change is a moving target that continues to diminish. A predicted drop from 25 to 3 to 1 foot in 15 years.[10]

Although some melting of the Earth's mid-latitude glaciers is taking place, these glaciers represent only 6% of the planet's total ice mass. The remaining 94 percent are expanding.[11] David Gorak reports, "The West Greenland Ice Sheet, the largest mass of polar ice in the Northern Hemisphere, has thickened by up to seven feet since 1980. It is highly unlikely that future global warming would melt polar glaciers enough to cause dramatic sea level change. The Antarctic ice sheet is very large and very cold; it would take the West Atlantic Ice Sheet 50,000 years to react to any warming that may be occurring today."[12]

John Christy, in writing about a *Time* article had this to say: "*Time* magazine, in a cover story in April 2001, declared that the Antarctic summer 'melt season has increased up to three weeks in 20 years.' Adelie penguins were suffering (of course, there was an accompanying photo of the adorable creatures, wings extended as if asking for help, when in fact they were sunning themselves in the frigid air). *Time* must have been thinking of temperatures at one tiny spot on this icebound continent. The data show that for the whole of Antarctica, the summer melt season is actually *decreasing* because the average surface temperature there had *declined* in the past 30 years. And new evidence suggests the ice cap is actually thickening after 10,000 years of thinning — a surprising result that contradicts the 'catastrophists' expectations."[13]

Global warming is also supposed to be causing a rise in the severity of coastal storms. Reliable records in the North Atlantic show that during the past fifty years the number of severe hurricanes has not increased and the average intensity of all hurricanes has weakened. Even the IPCC says, "Overall there is no evidence that extreme weather events, or climate variability, has increased, in a global sense, through the 20th century."[14]

The final assumed catastrophe of global warming is the dangerous effects on the health of humans. Wilfred Beckerman points out that the human race is not some tender plant that can only survive in a narrow temperature range. He cites these statistics for average temperatures in the coldest months; 32.3% of the world's population live in a band of 0 to 3 degrees Celsius, 18.8% live in the band 12 to 15 degrees Celsius, and 14.6% in a band 24 to 27 degrees Celsius. The same wide dispersion exists if one looks at summer temperatures.[15]

For most folks, a few degrees increase in temperature would probably improve health. Thomas Moore notes, "High death rates in the tropics appear to be more a function of poverty than of climate. Thus global warming is likely to prove positive for human health.[16] For those who worry about the increase of mosquito borne diseases with increasing temperature, the question should be asked, "Why aren't you concerned about the millions that die from malaria in our present times," since we persist in preventing the use of DDT? It's like, "let's not be worried about those dying right now, but let's worry about fictitious deaths in the future.

Now let's discuss the Kyoto Protocol. The middle range forecast, based on expected growth in fossil fuel use without any curbs is for a 1 degree Celsius increase in temperature between now and 2050. If Kyoto, which calls for a worldwide 5% cut in carbon dioxide emissions from 1990 levels was implemented and was successful, this would reduce the expected temperature insignificantly. How insignificant? Specifically, the reduction in temperature that would occur would make a mere six year difference. In other words, the temperature that we would reach in 2094 without a deal, would be postponed to 2100 with Kyoto.[17] We are being asked to spend an exorbitant amount of money for minuscule results.

Here's another fact to consider. Should the industrialized nations manage to stop or reverse carbon dioxide production, it would be of little importance, when, in the next century, many more billions of people will reach the same consumption levels the developed nations have today. Within the Kyoto Protocol, developing nations such as

China, India, Mexico, Brazil, South Korea, and Indonesia (to name a few), are exempt from following the rules of the treaty.[18]

To illustrate, let's look at China, which is exempt from Kyoto. If you have not noticed, China is booming. Once as poor as India, China has been transformed beyond recognition by two decades of roaring economic growth. Vast numbers of people have been lifted out of poverty and into middle class comfort.[19] China already consumes more energy and emits more greenhouse gases than any country except the United States. Moreover, China's recent breakneck pace of modernization already has left it with nine of the world's ten most polluted cities.[20]

Here are some other facts about China that make one ask why they should be excluded from the Kyoto treaty.

- After several years of strong growth, China is now the world's fourth-largest auto market, behind the U.S., Japan, and Germany. It could leap into second place in three years, even if growth continues at just half its current pace.[21]
- The Chinese are now graduating 700,000 engineers per year as compared with 60,000 per year in the United States.[22]
- China is poised to become the third country to launch humans into space after the safe return of its latest craft, which carried instrumented dummies.[23]
- China leads the world in cell phones with 150 million.[24]

China is now irreversibly on the road to Superpower status and thus will be a major factor in shaping the geopolitical dynamics of the 21st century. This doesn't sound like a third world country to me. Others will follow. Travel writer Jeff Greenwald says this, "During 15 years of travel writing I've seen places develop so rapidly that I simply can't bear to visit them again. And the most drastic changes, it seems, have occurred within the past decade."[25]

Global warming and climate research is big business in the United States. As of July 2001, the U.S. had spent $18 billion on climate research, which is three times as much as any other country, and more than Japan and the entire European Union combined.[26] When high funding stakes are involved, it could mean loss of sponsorship which would explain why many of the scientists who do not agree with the current global warming beliefs are not joining the discussion.

Daniel Grossman interviewed Richard S. Lindzen, who holds an endowed chair at the Massachusetts Institute of Technology, and was a lead author of one chapter of the Intergovernmental Panel on Climate Change (IPCC). The IPCC is "largely considered to be the definitive scientific assessment of climate change." Lindzen has this to say: "The country's leading scientists prefer not to wade into the troubled waters of climate change. It's the kind of pressure that the average scientist doesn't need." He adds, "It's not that humans have no effect at all on climate. They do, though with as much impact on the environment as when 'a butterfly shuts its wings.'"[27]

Lindzen has company. John Christy, a professor of atmospheric science at the University of Alabama in Huntsville is also a member of the IPCC. After interviewing Christy, Elizabeth Royte reports, "Years ago he cast doubt on the idea that global warming is caused by humans — or that the phenomenon exists at all — and he has only grown more skeptical as most other atmospheric scientists have grown more certain."[28]

It is interesting to also note that global warming has spawned a cottage industry in the nation's capital, courtesy of the Environmental Protection Agency. Via this agency, the federal government has funded almost $7 million to private groups that advocate the climate treaty.[29] The groups, which call themselves 'nongovernmental organizations,' clearly have much to gain from supporting global warming.

In the end, according to Robert Park, "Science is a wild card. The further we try to project ourselves into the future, the more certain it becomes that some unforeseen, perhaps unforeseeable, advance in science or technology will shuffle the deck before we get there."[30] In 1975 *Newsweek* wrote a horror story about the coming ice age complete with pronouncements from scientists who were studying the problem and who only needed more research money.[31] Richard Lindzen remembers that time. "The global cooling trend of the 1950s and 1960s led to a minor global cooling hysteria in the 1970s. All this was more or less scientific debate although the cooling hysteria had certain striking analogues to the present warming hysteria, including books such as *The Genesis Strategy* by Stephen Schneider and *Climate Change*

and World Affairs, by Crispin Ticknell (both authors are now prominent supporters of global warming) explaining the problem and pro-
moting international regulation."[32]

While on the subject of ice ages, some researchers are now predict-
ing that the next ice age could appear within ten years. The culprit?
Global warming. Logic seems to say, that a warmer planet cannot support an ice age, doesn't it? It seems that any statement, no matter how
illogical, is fair game to keep the agenda rolling.

Is it really worth all the money and worry we are putting into this
issue? Perhaps our focus and dollars are spent better elsewhere. Bjorn
Lomborg reports that the cost of the Kyoto treaty, "just for the U.S.,
will be higher than the cost of providing the entire world with clean
drinking water and sanitation. It is estimated that the latter would
avoid two million deaths every year and prevent half a billion people
becoming seriously ill every year."[33] Indur Goklany adds, "Consid-
ering that a million Africans die from malaria annually, and that it
costs $8 to save a life-year from malaria, humanity would be better
served if a billion dollars were spent to reduce malaria (and the potentially climate-sensitive diseases) in the immediate future rather than
spending ten, if not hundreds, of billions to limit climate change that
may or may not reduce the burden of disease decades from now."[34]

To close this chapter, let's reiterate how much warmer the globe
became during the last century. Just one-half a degree Celsius or 0.9
degrees Fahrenheit over a 100 year period.

References

1.   John R. Christy, "The Global Warming Fiasco," in *Global Warming and Other
     Eco-Myths*, Ronald Bailey, Editor, (Roseville, CA, Forum, Prima Publishing
     Co., 2002), 1

2.   *A Guide to Global Warming*, (Washington, D.C., George C. Marshall Insti-
     tute, January 2000), 4

3.   *A Guide to Global Warming*, (Washington, D.C., George C. Marshall Insti-
     tute, January 2000), 2

4.   Robert H. Essenhigh, "Does CO_2 really drive global warming?", *Chemical
     Innovation*, 31, 44 (May 2001)

5. James P. Collman, *Naturally Dangerous*, (Sausalito, CA, University Science Books, 2001), 181

6. C.R. de Freitas, "Are observed changes in the concentration of carbon dioxide in the atmosphere really dangerous?", *Bulletin of Canadian Petroleum Geology*, 50, 297 (2002)

7. Robert C. Balling, Jr., "Global Warming: The Gore Version Versus Climate Reality,: in *Environmental Gore: A Constructive Response to Earth in the Balance,"*, John A. Baden, Editor, (San Francisco, CA, Pacific Research Institute for Public Policy, 1995), 109

8. Jay H. Lehr, "It's the sun," (Ostrander, OH, Environmental Education Enterprises, January 18, 2002)

9. "Global Warming in Brief," Global Warming Information Page, www.globalwarming.org, (February 7, 2003)

10. "The Global Warming Crisis: Predictions of Warming Continue to Drop," in *Facts on Global Warming*, (Washington, D.C., George C. Marshall Institute, October 15, 1997)

11. Aaron Wildavsky, *"But is it True? A Citizen's Guide to Environmental Health and Safety Issues*, (Cambridge Massachusetts, Harvard University Press, 1995), 368

12. David Gorak, "Glacier melting: Just a drop in the bucket," *Environment & Climate News*, 2, 6 (May 1999)

13. John R. Christy, "The Global Warming Fiasco," in *Global Warming and Other Eco-Myths*, Ronald Bailey, Editor, (Roseville, CA, Forum, Prima Publishing Co., 2002), 4

14. "Will Global Warming Cause an Increase in Hurricanes and Severe Storms?", in *Facts on Global Warming*, (Washington, D.C., George C. Marshall Institute, November 19, 1997)

15. Wilfred Beckerman, *Green-Colored Glasses*, (Washington, D.C., Cato Institute, 1996), 105

16. Thomas Gale Moore, *Climate of Fear*, (Washington, D.C., Cato Institute, 1998), 88

17. Bjorn Lomborg, *The Skeptical Environmentalist*, (Cambridge, Cambridge University Press, 2001), 302

18. Eugene M. Trisko, "The Global Warming Game: China 1, US Workers 0," National Center for Policy Analysis, NCPA-BA #239 (August 20, 1997)

19.   "The Great Race," *The Economist*, July 6, 2002, page 3

20.   Environmental Change & Security Project Report, Woodrow Wilson International Center for Scholars, Issue No. 8, (Summer 2002), 267

21.   Karby Leggett and Todd Zaun, "World's Car Makers Race to Keep Up With China Boom," *Wall Street Journal*, December 13, 2002, A1

22.   Arthur B. Robinson, *Access to Energy*, 30, 2 (November 2002)

23.   Ding Yimin and Dennis Normile, "Human Flight is Next Step for China's Space Program," *Science*, 299, 180 (January 10, 2003)

24.   Billy O. Wireman, "China's 21st Century Educational Challenge," *Vital Speeches*, Volume LXIX, 187 (January 1, 2003)

25.   Jeff Greenwald, *Scratching the Surface*, (Oakland, CA, Naga Books, 2002), 148

26.   George W. Bush, "Global Climate Change," *Vital Speeches of the Day*, Volume LXVII, 546 (July 1, 2001)

27.   Daniel Grossman, "Dissent in the Maelstrom," *Scientific American*, 285, 38 (November 2001)

28.   Elizabeth Royte, "The Gospel According to John," *Discover*, 22, 66, (February 2001)

29.   "Cashing in on Global Warming," Global Warming Information Page, www.globalwarming.org, (February 7, 2003)

30.   Robert Park, *Voodoo Science*, (Oxford, Oxford University Press, 2000), 87

31.   "The cooling world, *Newsweek*, April 28, 1975, 64

32.   Richard S. Lindzen, "Global Warming: The Origin and Nature of Alleged Scientific Consensus," in *Environmental Gore: A Constructive Response to Earth in the Balance*, John A. Baden, editor, (San Francisco, CA, Pacific Research Institute for Public Policy, 1995), 123

33.   Bjorn Lomborg, *The Skeptical Environmentalist*, 318

34.   Indur M. Goklany, *The Precautionary Principle*, (Washington, D.C., Cato Institute, 2001), 81

Section 2:

Chemicals — The Other Side of the Story

Chapter 6

Chemophobia

When Alice Ottoboni published the first edition of her book *The Dose Makes The Poison* in 1984, she said that she thought the public's fear of environmental chemicals had peaked. In 1991, when she published the second edition, she acknowledged that time had proved her wrong and poison paranoia had continued to flourish. "The general public," she said, "seems more concerned than ever about environmental chemicals." Again responding to public paranoia about chemicals, she updated the book in 1997.[1]

Some of this negative thinking is due to chemophobia, the fear of chemicals and our concern about chemicals and cancer. This, combined with increasing government and industry recognition that people must be protected from harmful exposures has caused a dramatic increase during the past 20 years in the number of laws regulating chemicals. Policymakers in the United States are so obsessed with the fear of manmade chemicals that they spend $31 billion annually, money that could be spent more effectively on other lifesaving programs.[2]

There is also a quality of life cost. In the preface of her book, *Endangered Pleasures*, Barbara Holland says, "Subtly, in little ways, joy has been leaking out of our lives. Almost without a struggle, we have allowed the spreading of a layer of foreboding across the land. Perhaps we have some guilt over our material success, and that makes us worry that our success is either undeserved or only temporary. Perhaps our Calvinistic roots have led us to believe that pain is more noble than pleasure, thus rendering us susceptible to arguments that everything we eat, drink, breath, touch or see might hurt us. Whatever the reason, bad news always travels faster and seems more credible than good news."[3]

For many years the media has deluged the public with sensational reports that cancer risk is on the rise because our food, air and water contain traces of artificially produced carcinogens.[4] Mostly the reports are unjustified by facts. The percentage of cancers induced by synthetic chemicals is so low that it cannot be measured reliably enough to verify, while the cancer-causing effects of banning chemicals, such as diminished consumption of fruits and vegetables, are high and easily measurable.[5] In other words, if we stop eating fruits and vegetables that we believe were sprayed with cancer-causing pesticides or preservatives, we are increasing our chance of getting cancer more than ingesting of the trace amounts of chemicals.

So what's the deal? Every piece of food we eat, every breath we take, every move we make results in the ingestion of a chemical of some sort. Every chemical has the ability to kill, but only if the quantities are high enough. As the Swiss physician Paracelsus stated: "What is not poison? All things are poison and nothing is without poison. It is only the dose that makes a thing a poison."

The principle put forth by Paracelsus is detailed in the following table.[6]

Lethal dose of certain chemicals in a number of foods[a]

Chemical	Lethal Dose
Caffeine	100 cups of coffee
Solanine	100-400 pounds of potatoes
Oxalic acid	10-20 pounds spinach or rhubarb
Hydrogen cyanide	3.7 pounds of lima beans
Malonaldehyde	3.8 tons of turkey
Acetyl salicylic acid	100 aspirin tablets
Water	17 liters in a very short time

(a) M. Alice Ottoboni, *The Dose Makes the Poison*, (New York, John Wiley & Sons, 1997), 43

I challenge anyone to eat 3.7 pounds of lima beans in one sitting. Although there are lethal chemicals in the food we eat, it is important to realize that we ingest many "lethal doses" of a wide variety of compounds but they have no effect on us because we spread the dose over a lifetime. Also, normal diets don't create risk, because our body chemistry quickly flushes these compounds through them.[7]

For example, in consuming the average 119 pounds of potatoes each year, we take into our system approximately 9,700 milligrams of solanine, enough to literally kill a horse. But it really doesn't matter because we don't eat that much at one time. There appears to be three reasons why toxic, or potentially toxic substances pose no hazard under the usual conditions of consumption: (1) the levels are usually too low to have an effect; (2) individual chemicals appear not to be additive, that is, two or three different toxic substances in potatoes or lima beans or another source do not "add up" to make a hazard, and; (3) there is evidence that the toxicity of one element is often offset by the presence of an adequate amount of another.[8]

Bruce Ames and his colleagues have shown that many of our foods contain pesticides created naturally by plants for self-protection. We ingest at least 10,000 times more, by weight, of natural pesticides than of synthetic pesticide residues. These natural toxic chemicals vary enormously in chemical structure, appear to be present in all plants, and serve to protect plants against fungi, insects, and animal predators.[9]

William Baarschers notes: "The emphasis on pesticides that started with *Silent Spring* and subsequent literature on the topic had a profound effect on the way people think about food. A very large body of knowledge about food and food chemicals has almost been forgotten or is ignored."[10] Suffice to say, there is probably no food that does not contain some potentially harmful natural chemical. This fact is the basis for an annual project of the American Council on Science and Health (ACSH) which publishes a typical holiday dinner menu each year identifying the naturally occuring toxic or carcinogenic chemicals present in each food. Below is a look at a sample menu and the chemicals contained (again, **naturally**) in the food.[11]

1.   Cream of Mushroom Soup
2.   Fresh Vegetable Tray (Carrots, Radishes, Cherry Tomatoes, Celery)
3.   Roast Turkey
4.   Cranberry Sauce
5.   Cooked Vegetables (Lima beans, broccoli spears, baked potato)
6.   Pumpkin and Apple Pie
7.   Coffee, Tea, Red Wine

Hydrazines, carotatoxin, myristicin, isoflavones, nitrate, hydrogen peroxide, quercetin, glycosides, tomatine, psolarens, heterocyclic amines, malonaldehyde, eugenol, furan derivatives, cyanogenetic glycosides, ally isothiocyanate, glucosinates, goitrin, amylase inhibitors, arsenic, chaconine, isoflavones, oxalic acid, solanine, safrole, acetaldehyde, phlorizin, benzo(a)pyrene, caffeine, tannins, alcohol, ethyl carbamate, methylglyoxal, tyramine.

As the ACSH points out in the notes accompanying the annual menu, their purpose in "not to frighten our already chemophobic nation, but to empasize the reality that humans have long been consuming potentially toxic substances that occur naturally. It is time for the American people to stop acting on the presumption that 'natural' is safe and 'man-made' is suspect.[11]

Besides food, we are exposed to a variety of chemicals in air and water. Air is a mixture of 16 primary natural constituents and countless "trace" substances which vary with time and location. A recent review listed over 100 organic chemicals found in rain water, along with various inorganic salts and dissolved gases.[12]

I guess the simplest answer to our chemophobia is this. It is based on a misperception. EVERYTHING IS MADE UP OF CHEMICALS. A 1983 report by the National Research Council noted that about 5,000,000 different chemical substances are known to exist.[13] Of those five million, less than 30 have been definitively linked to cancer in humans, 1500 have been found to be carcinogenic in tests on animals, and about 7000 have been tested for carcinogenity. Again, if you missed those numbers, less than 30 out of five million known chemical substances have been definitively linked to cancer in humans.

What are we so worried about? Our worries are without reality, and yet our chemophobia continues to grow, as does our willingness to place blame. As Anthony Michaelis states: "The main attack has been directed against industry, particularly the multinational chemical manufacturers, which are accused of placing profits before environmental considerations. In many cases, industry, for obvious reasons, has remained silent when accused, which is interpreted as a cover up."[14] Further, scientists who work for chemical corporations have little credibility with the public and a recent poll shows that only tobacco companies are more distrusted than chemical companies. That's pretty bad, but perhaps the chemists must share the blame with the media for their standing.

"Chemistry is an exceedingly difficult subject to popularize in the press," says Michaelis. It is also difficult to explain. One reason the public is not better informed about chemicals is that many scientists do not communicate well with the public and when they do, they are ineffective. The press and the media can always find a naysayer scientist (or non-scientist) to discuss the latest cancer scare, but all too often the rest of the story is not being told. Scientists and engineers must speak out to correct misinformation and state the facts in a consumer friendly and understanding manner. Melvin Benarde has pointed out that scientists have simply attended their meetings, read their papers, and gone home, satisfied they have done a good day's work. He says that this is "patently unsatisfactory and leaves the door open for muckrakers with their purple prose and clever amateurs who cry "poison."[15]

Some phobias are based on things that are truly scary (arachnophobia is a good personal example), but chemophobia here in the United States (and spreading) is often based on misperception, mistrust, and mistruth.

References

1.   M. Alice Ottoboni, *The Dose Makes The Poison*, First Edition, (Berkeley, Vicente Books, Berkeley, 1984), Second Edition, (New York, Van Nostrand Reinhold, 1991), and (New York, John Wiley & Sons, 1997)

2.   James Walsh, *True Odds*, (Santa Monica, California, Merritt Publishing, 1996), 99

3.   B. Holland, *Endangered Pleasures*, (New York, Little, Brown & Co., 1995)

4.   Merrill Eisenbud, *How Clean is Clean? How Safe is Safe?*, (Madison, Wisconsin, Cogito Books, 1993), 27

5.   Bruce N. Ames, Renae Magaw, and Lois Swirsky Gold, "Ranking Possible Carcinogenic Hazards," *Science*, 236, (April 17, 1987), 271

6.   M. Alice Ottoboni, *The Dose Makes The Poison*, (New York, John Wiley & Sons, 1997), 43

7.   American Council on Science and Health, "Environmental Chemicals: Public Health Concern or PR Hype?" (October 1996)

8.   Elizabeth M. Whelan and Frederick J. Stare, *Panic in the Pantry*, (New York, Atheneum, 1975), 100 and 104

9. Bruce N. Ames and Lois Swirsky Gold, "Environmental Pollution and Cancer: Some Misconceptions," in *Rational Readings on Environmental Concerns*, ed. Jay H. Lehr, (New York, Van Nostrand Reinhold, 1992), 153

10. William H. Baarschers, *Eco-Facts & Eco-Fiction*, (London, Routledge, 1996), 40

11. American Council on Science and Health, "Holiday Dinner Menu-1992"

12. *Chemicals in the Human Food Chain*, eds., Carl K. Winter, James N. Seiber and Carole F. Nuckton, (New York, Van Nostrand Reinhold, 1990), 181

13. John Adams, *Risk*, (London, University College Press, 1995), 45

14. Anthony R. Michaelis, "Stop-Chemophobia," *Interdisciplinary Science Reviews*, 21, (1996), 130

15. Melvin A. Benarde, *The Chemicals We Eat*, (New York, American Heritage Press, 1971), 184

Chapter 7

Poopophobia

Are you worried that everything you eat, drink, breathe and touch might hurt you? If so, you may suffer from chemophobia, the fear of chemicals and your concern about chemicals causing cancer. Well, I'm gonna toss a new phobia at you, which has much more substance than chemophobia. Hey, if you are going to expend energy worrying, it should be spent here.

Poopophobia.

Experts at the Food and Drug Administration (FDA) decide on how much contamination is to be allowed in foods sold for human consumption. There is no question regarding "how much" since it would be impossible to produce food that had no contaminants whatsoever. Here are some of the FDA guidelines for maximum permissible levels of certain "impurities."

Contaminants in Food[a]

Brussel sprouts	10 aphids per ounce
Shelled peanuts	1 insect per 5 pounds
Golden raisins	4 fly eggs per ounce
Tomato juice	3 fly eggs per ounce
Whole peppercorns	1 percent mammalian excreta
Popcorn	2 rodent hairs per pound
Fig paste	4 insect heads per ounce
Peanut butter	9 insect fragments per ounce
Canned mushrooms	5 maggots per ounce

a. Larry Laudan, *Danger Ahead*, (New York, John Wiley & Sons, 1997), 88

Looking at the chart, you can agree with Larry Laudan who stated, "It's quite a facer to realize that up to 1 in every 100 peppercorns we grind over our food could be a rat turd."[1] With chemicals, we talk about a few parts per million, parts per billion, or even parts per trillion. With animal excreta (rat turds, mite turds, ant turds, etc.), my math says that one part per 100 is equivalent to 10,000 parts per million, now these are some serious parts per million. Sure, some folks will tell you that insect parts are not a health hazard, and as the Berkeley Wellness Letter says, "if you're feeling philosophical you might reflect that they provide a bit of protein."[2] But turds?

Here's some more information on poop and bugs.

· Some foods contain a coloring agent called cochineal extract or carmine which is derived from a type of mealybug found on cacti. The red dye from cochineal is used to add color to juices, yogurts, fruit fillings, and a host of other foods, as well as some cosmetics and lipstick. As the Berkeley Wellness Letter reports: "Cochineal extract is natural and harmless, is always processed to destroy any bacterial contamination, and is approved as a food coloring by the FDA. It's not ground up bugs, but simply the color extracted from them. But some strict vegetarians want no part of any insect, not even a red molecule in their food. Furthermore, insects are not kosher, so cochineal may bring up religious concerns."[2]

· Edward Tenner notes the following: "The fecal pellets of dust mites contain a powerful allergen, Der pI, which stimulates the immune system to inflame the airways. A study of children growing up in England showed that those from houses with high levels of dust-mite allergens were up to five times more likely as others to become asthmatic by their teens. Researchers estimated that children were being exposed to as many as 500,000 fecal particles per gram of house dust."[3]

· A senior veterinary scientist believes that domestic pets may be passing E.coli O157 bacteria to their home owners. The organism caused a food poisoning outbreak in central Scotland in 1996, killing 21 people. In 1999 there were 1,000 poisoning cases in England and Wales caused by O157, the highest number ever recorded. Says Professor Mac Johnson of the UK's Royal Veterinary College, "Domestic animals are very likely to pick up O157 from the environment. And equally, as it comes out the other end in their droppings they will be passing it on. So anything that's attractive to children, like the tail of a dog, is potentially a source of O157 for them. I don't know why we've had no cases linked with it. I suspect it could just be a matter of time before the link is proven."[4]

- Pets may also be a major cause of water pollution in urban areas, particularly following periods of heavy rain say researchers at Vanderbilt University.[5] They measured levels of fecal coliform in four neighborhoods in north Nashville, Tennessee and found high bacteria levels in runoff from streets and lawns. "We can't say with absolute certainty that pets, along with other urban wildlife, are the cause of this bacterial pollution," says one of the coauthors, "but all signs point in that direction." The researchers found that the higher the housing density in the neighborhood, the higher the level of contamination, and one of the things associated with housing density is the number of pets per acre. In reviewing the research, David Salisbury noted: "Two factors contribute to the pet pollution problem. One is the sheer number of pets in urban areas. The density of pets in urban neighborhoods is far greater than the number of similarly sized animals in a wild setting. The second is the nature of the urban environment itself. In the wild, animal droppings are generally held in place where they fall by long grass or bushes. This allows them to decompose in place. By comparison, streets, parking lots, and even lawns are hard, flat surfaces. So animal wastes deposited there are less likely to decompose and much more likely to get washed into drains and ditches and carried into nearby streams."[6]

- Alex Kirby reports, "Colonies of seabirds are adding to environmental pollution simply by doing what comes naturally. The birds are releasing large amounts of ammonia into the atmosphere through their droppings. Researchers say some species, such as gannets and guillemots, are guiltier than others. Very large emissions of ammonia could have a detrimental impact on the local ecology and may be just as problematic as intensive farming. Scientists studying a seabird colony on Bass Rock off the east coast of Scotland have already measured ammonia concentrations 20 times higher than those on chicken farms."[7]

- A pollution scare that baffled scientists and led to the closing of a popular Florida beach at the height of summer in 2000 was tentatively linked to the feces of a large flock of pigeons.[8]

- New Zealand scientists are alarmed by measurements showing that 44% of the nation's "greenhouse gases" result from methane production by sheep. They are actually proposing to breed sheep that emit less methane.[9]

Over 5,000 people die annually from foodborne illness, and more than 25 million people are hospitalized for acute gastroenteritis from food poisoning by unknown agents. Approximately 3,360 deaths, or 65% of those attributable to food poisonings, trace to unknown agents.[10] We know how to trace the chemicals, so they can't be blamed. Could it be bugs or poop?

References

1. Larry Laudan, *Danger Ahead*, (New York, John Wiley & Sons, 1997), 88

2. "Don't Let This Bug You," *University of California at Berkeley Wellness Letter*, 14, (March 1998), 6

3. Edward Tenner, *Why Things Bite Back*, (New York, Alfred A. Knopf, 1996), 103

4. Alex Kirby, "E. coli risk from family pets," *BBC News Online*, (May 4, 2000), http://bbc.co.uk/

5. Katherine D. Young and Edward L. Thackston, "Housing Density and Bacterial Loading in Urban Streams," *Journal of Environmental Engineering*, 125 (December 1999), 1177

6. David F. Salisbury, "Pets may be a major cause of water pollution in urban areas," Vanderbilt University (December 3, 1999) www.vanderbilt.edu

7. Alex Kirby, "The innocent polluters," *BBC News Online*, (March 8, 2000), http://bbc.co.uk/

8. Steve Milloy, (July 24, 2000), www.junkscience.com

9. Arthur B. Robinson, Access to Energy, 29, 4 (February 2002)

10. Janet Raloff, "What Are the Causes of Foodborne Illness?", *Consumer's Research*, 83, (January 2000), 28

Chapter 8

DDT: The Real Story

DDT (Dichlorodiphenyltrichloroethane). Here's what you have heard about this firebrand pesticide. It nearly wiped out the bald eagle and the peregrine falcon populations in the United States because it causes egg-shell thinning. It is a carcinogen, mutagen, and teratogen. DDT stays in the environment for extremely long periods of time, constantly poisoning soil, water, and wildlife. For all these reasons, DDT was banned from use in the United States in 1972.

This ban was considered the first major victory of the environmental movement, and has been heralded as such for the past 30 years. Certainly this was an important victory that has saved the planet from catastrophe?

No.

The DDT ban is one of the most horrific acts in history. Since DDT was banned, the incidence of malaria has increased enormously worldwide and the disease has risen from the ashes to again be a leading cause of death. Every 30 seconds, a child dies of malaria.[1] The use of DDT had brought the number of malaria cases (and fatalities) to the lowest numbers in history as it controlled the Anopheles mosquito populations. We'll look at the numbers later in the chapter.

Now, you might be saying "if we had continued to use DDT, the incidence of death and sickness would be much higher because it is so dangerous." Sorry, but DDT got a bad rap, and all the scientific evidence was cast to the side of the road by politics. The decision to ban DDT was based on emotion, hysteria, and politics, not on science.

Let's take a look at the history of DDT and the decision to engage the ban on its usage, and then take a look at the truth about DDT **based on science**.

Early in the 1900s, the only effective way to control malaria was to eliminate stagnant water, such as in swamps and landfills, where Anopheles mosquitoes breed. In 1942, DDT was shown to kill body lice without adverse effect on humans, and it was used by Allied troops in World War II. No Allied soldier was stricken with typhus fever (carried by lice) marking the first time in the history of warfare that soldiers had thus been spared. In contrast, during World War I, three million people died of typhus in Russia and Eastern Europe, and more soldiers died from typhus than from gunfire.[2] DDT became available in 1943 and its use spread worldwide as it was extremely effective, and was not cost-prohibitive.

The downfall of DDT began in 1962 when Rachel Carson's best seller, *Silent Spring*, indicted DDT as a killer of birds, fish, and wildlife.[3] This eventually led to a long (7 months) federal hearing in 1972 on the risks and benefits of the material. The hearings were ordered by EPA Administrator William Ruckelshaus, who appointed Judge Edmund Sweeney as the hearing examiner. After 150 expert scientific witnesses, review of 300 technical documents, and over 9,000 pages of testimony, Judge Sweeney concluded the following: DDT is not a carcinogenic, mutagenic, or teratogenic hazard to man; the use of DDT under the registrations involved does not have a deleterious effect on fish, estuarine organisms, wild birds, or other wildlife.[4,5]

In a better world, this would have been good news. It was met instead with journalistic and environmental hysteria across the nation. Less than two months after the hearing, Ruckleshaus single-handedly banned almost all use of DDT. No reasons were given at the time, but as Dixy Lee Ray and Lou Guzzo report: "Years later, Ruckelshaus admitted that decisions by the government involving the use of toxic substances are political and ultimate judgment remains political. In the case of pesticides, the power to make this judgment has been delegated to the Administrator of the EPA."[4] As mentioned earlier, this ban on DDT was considered the first major victory for the environmentalist movement in the United States.[6] "It gave credibility to pseudoscience, it created an atmosphere in which scientific evidence can be pushed aside by emotion, hysteria, and political pressure. It has done inestimable damage. The technique of making unsubstantiated charges, endlessly repeated, has since been used successfully against asbestos, PCBs, dioxin, and of course, Alar."[7]

Let's take a look at "unsubstantiated charges" and the actual scientific evidence.

In *Silent Spring*, Rachel Carson started the DDT ball rolling by stating that the American robin was on the verge of extinction. That same year, Roger Tory Peterson, America's leading ornithologist, wrote that the robin was most likely the most numerous North American Bird.[8] Carson's notion that the most prolific bird was about to fall extinct was one of the most eye-catching assertions in *Silent Spring* and brought the book considerable publicity. Peregrine falcons and eagles were also high on Carson's list of endangered species. Reporting on population declines in these species, she heaped the blame on pesticides and ignored all data that would refute her theory.[9] Peregrine falcons were extremely rare in the eastern United States long before DDT was present. By the time DDT was introduced there were literally no peregrine falcon populations in the eastern United States but the anti-pesticide extremists later blamed DDT for their absence anyway.[10] Bald eagles were on the verge of extinction in the lower 48 states in the 1920s and 1930s, long before DDT was developed. They were shot on sight for fun, bounty, or feathers, trapped accidentally, killed by impact with buildings and towers, or electrocuted by power lines. Eagles still fall victim to these physical hazards, but much less to shooting and trapping due to stiff prison terms for those engaging in these activities. The bald eagle population has rebounded. The most surprising thing though, is that environmental folks and the news media continue to attribute the increase to just one thing, the 1972 ban on DDT.[11]

Even the oft-repeated claim that DDT causes birds to lay eggs with dangerously thin shells falls apart under close inspection. DDT opponents alleged then and now that DDT causes the eggshells of certain birds to become thin or soft; as a consequence, eggs fail to hatch and populations decline.

Thin eggshells are a phenomenon that predated the use of DDT. We've known about them for decades and there are many causes: diets low in calcium or Vitamin D, fright, high or low daily temperatures, and bird maladies such as Newcastle disease.[12] Caged experiments have repeatedly demonstrated that DDT and its breakdown products do not cause significant shell thinning, even at levels many hundreds of times greater that any wild bird would accumulate.[13] The most notorious cause of thin eggshells is calcium deficiency. An early researcher working with quails deliberately fed them only calcium-deficient food (containing 0.5% rather than the necessary 2.5% calcium) and then attributed all shell problems to the DDT and DDE they had added to that diet. Edwards reports that after much criticism about these deceptive practices, the researchers repeated the tests, but with adequate calcium in the birds' diet. The results proved that with sufficient calcium in their food, the quail produced eggs with normal shells.[14]

Another way to obtain data is to measure the thickness of eggshells in museum collections. Measurements of hundreds of museum eggs have revealed that red-tailed hawks eggs produced just before DDT was introduced had much thinner shells than did eggs produced ten years earlier. "Then, during the years of heavy DDT usage, those hawks produced shells that were 6% thicker. Golden eagle eggshells during the DDT years were 5% thicker that those produced before DDT was present in the environment.[15] More recently, Rhys E. Green found that thrush eggshells in Great Britain were thinning before the turn of the last century, 47 years before DDT hit the market. He speculates that the thinning may have been an early consequence of industrialization. "Acids formed when pollutants belch out of coal furnaces and smokestacks may have changed the soil and water chemistry enough to reduce the availability of calcium, which is critical for eggshells."[16]

Many environmental contaminants do cause egg shell thinning, including oil, lead, mercury, cadmium, lithium, manganese, selenium and sulfur compounds. PCBs have been shown to cause dramatic thinning of eggshells, as well as other adverse effects on birds. Yet, environmentalists continued to place the blame on DDT despite the fact that feeding birds high levels of that pesticide did not cause them to produce thin eggshells.[17] Ms. Carson's book, not based in any way on scientific fact, started an emotional firestorm that as we will discuss later can be linked to millions of deaths worldwide.

Regarding toxicity, I will first mention that in almost all references on toxic and hazardous chemicals DDT is listed as a carcinogen. This is certainly because DDT continues via political pressure to be considered as such. However, DDT is known to be safe to humans. As Edward Tenner reports: "Even workers with heavy, prolonged exposure

seemed to suffer no ill effects. Only one case of a directly lethal exposure is known: some DDT powder, confused with flour, was cooked in
pancakes."[18] In controlled studies of human volunteers, experimental ingestion of 35 milligrams of DDT per kilogram of body weight per
day, for a period of two years, produced no adverse effects, acute or
chronic, in any of the subjects.[19] Doses of five grams of DDT (and
even more) have been administered to human beings in the successful
treatment of barbituate poisoning according to Walter Ebeling, professor of entomology at UCLA.[20] J. Gordon Edwards reported in a
study of workers at the Montrose Chemical Company, a producer of
DDT: "workers used no gloves or protective clothing of any kind and
were inhaling DDT dust all day. It is noteworthy that (after 10 to 20
years on the job) no cases of cancer developed among these workers in
some 1,300 man-years of exposure, a statistically improbable event."[21]

One of the more interesting examples verifying that DDT is non-
toxic to humans is the experience of J. Gordon Edwards, Professor of
Biology at San Jose State University. Says Edwards, "After remembering my own days of dusting hundreds of civilians during the war in
Europe with 10% DDT to kill lice and help prevent millions of cases
of deadly typhus, I thought I should try to convince people that environmental extremists were wrong. Thereafter, at the beginning of
each DDT speech I made, I would publicly eat a tablespoon of DDT
powder. It resulted in a full page photograph of me doing that in
Esquire magazine (September 1971). The caption stated that I was
eating 200 times the normal intake of DDT to show it's not as bad as
people think."[22] Today, as Edwards approaches his 84th birthday, he
is still as adamantly opposed to the anti-DDT propaganda as he was
over 30 years ago. An avid climber, Edwards continues to conquer
peaks greater than 10,000 feet. DDT exposure surely hasn't hurt him.

In 1969, rodent studies suggested DDT was a carcinogen. However, these results were refuted by a 1978 National Cancer Institute
report that concluded, after two years of testing on several different
strains of cancer prone mice and rats, that DDT was not carcinogenic.[23] More recently, Robert Golden, a Ph.D. toxicologist in
Potomac, Maryland stated: "the one endocrine modulator environmentalists love to hate, the pesticide DDT, would cause no endocrine
effect in a fetus exposed to more than a pound of DDT over the course
of a pregnancy.[24]

It is worth noting that the pesticides that replaced DDT, organo-phosphates such as parathion and malathion are far more deadly to humans. These chemicals belong to the same family as nerve gas and have caused serious poisoning, often fatal, among unsuspecting farm workers who had been accustomed to handling DDT.[25]

Another often heard claim about DDT is that it cannot be broken down in the environment. Actually, DDT is broken down rather rapidly by heat, cold, moisture, sunlight, alkalinity, salinity, soil micro-organisms, hepatic enzymes of birds and mammals, and a great many other environmental factors.[26] Only in unusual circumstances where soil is dark, dry and devoid of microorganisms will DDT persist. Under normal environmental conditions, DDT loses its toxicity to insects in a few days.[27] If it did not break down, it would be unnecessary to apply it again in order to control pests. Edwards provides a list of more than 140 articles documenting the breakdown of DDT in the environment.[28]

A key reason that traces of DDT are sometimes still found in environmental samples is that (as mentioned in previous chapters) we can now detect extremely minute amounts of anything. In the span of about two decades, detection limits have been increased by about six orders of magnitude.[29]

Some analysts have even reported DDT in samples collected before DDT existed. For example, University of Wisconsin chemists were given 34 soil samples to analyze. They reported that 32 of the 34 samples contained DDT. What the chemists did not know was that the soil samples had been hermetically sealed in 1911, and no DDT existed in the United States until 1940.[30,31] The apparent insecticides were actually misidentifications caused by the presence of co-extracted indigenous soil components. Still later, it was found that red algae also produces halogen compounds that are misidentified as DDT by gas chromatography. Also, halogen compounds containing bromine or iodine, rather than chlorine, may falsely register as DDT on the gas chromatograph.[32] Various PCBs were commonly misidentified as chlorinated hydrocarbon insecticides during the 1950s and 1960s, and were routinely reported as "DDT residues."

So, to this point, DDT has been proven to be safe for both the environment, and for humans. All the conjecture and rhetoric of the environmentalists has been shown as such, all based on emotion, hysteria, and pseudoscience. There is no real evidence to back their claims. Yet, President Bush has endorsed the Stockholm Convention on Persistent Organic Pollutants, the so-called "Dirty Dozen" which would ban DDT use worldwide. In doing so, we take part in the massive, ongoing negligent homicide of millions.

As mentioned earlier, every 30 seconds, a child dies of malaria, a problem that can be solved by the use of DDT. If environmentalists care so much about leaving a clean planet for our children, why do they ignore the fact that the children they want to leave the planet for are dying from a solvable problem? There are 300-500 million cases and three million deaths occuring annually, mostly in children. Worldwide, only AIDS and tuberculosis cause more deaths.[33] However, malaria had been all but beaten by DDT throughout the world.

"India had more than 100 million cases of malaria annually in the 1940s and 2.5 million people died of malaria each year. After a DDT spraying program had been implemented, that casualty rate had dropped to fewer than 100,000 cases and fewer than 1,000 deaths. Ceylon (now Sri Lanka) in the early 1950s had suffered 3 million cases of malaria annually, with more than 12,000 deaths. DDT spraying began in 1946 and by 1962 there were only 21 cases total, and the next year only 17 (with no deaths)."[34]

In 1969, the World Health Assembly (WHO) urged manufacturers to continue production of DDT, perceiving the potential threat to the world populus saying: "A ban on the production of DDT in the United States would deny the use of DDT to most of the malarious areas of the world. The direct result of such a denial would be to bring down upon the afflicted countries hundreds of millions of cases of malaria, and millions of deaths from malaria within the next decade."[35]

As Leonard Flynn reports, WHO was absolutely right. "In 1969, five years after DDT spraying stopped, the number of malaria cases in Ceylon had grown to over 500,000.[36] The numbers are crushing, from 17 total cases to over half a million in seven years. In South America, where DDT spraying has been continued until more recent times, data from 1993 to 1995 showed that countries recently discontinuing their spray programs are reporting large increases in malaria incidence. The only country in South America where malaria rates have gone down (by 61%) was Ecuador, which has increased the use of DDT since 1993.[37]

Since Rachel Carson's *Silent Spring*, a book with facts disputed by experts from the Audubon Society, claimed that DDT was responsible for the near extinction of several species, this highly effective and benign pesticide has been given a bad rap. Politicians, who rarely ever use actual science as a basis for legislation have banned this substance in the United States, and now are trying to ensure that it is banned everywhere in the world. There is no real evidence that DDT causes any of the problems that the environmentalists claim, yet because it is popular to do so, DDT remains part of the "dirty dozen." In ensuring that DDT cannot be used, and because there is no real alternative, millions of people have died, and millions more will continue to suffer and die of malaria, a problem that had been contained by this pesticide.

References

1. Donovan Webster, "Malaria Kills One Child Every 30 Seconds," *Smithsonian*, 31, (September 2000), 32

2. J. Gordon Edwards, "Malaria: The Killer That Could Have Been Conquered," *21st Century*, 6, (Summer 1993), 21

3. Rachel Carson, *Silent Spring*, (Greenwich, Connecticut, Fawcett Publications, 1962)

4. Dixy Lee Ray and Lou Guzzo, *Trashing the Planet*, (New York, Harper Perennial, 1992), 73

5. J. Gordon Edwards, "DDT Effects on Bird Abundance and Reproduction," in *Rational Readings on Environmental Concerns*, ed. Jay H. Lehr, (New York, Van Nostrand Reinhold, 1992), 208

6. Adam J. Lieberman, "DDT, 1962" in *Facts Versus Fear*, (New York, American Council on Science and Health, September 1997), 4

7. Dixy Lee Ray and Lou Guzzo, *Trashing the Planet*, 74

8. Thomas H. Jukes, "The Tragedy of DDT," in *Rational Readings on Environmental Concerns*, ed. Jay H. Lehr, (New York, Van Nostrand Reinhold, 1992), 217

9.   Melvin J. Grayson and Thomas R. Shepard, Jr., *The Disaster Lobby*, (Chicago, Follett Publishing Company, 1973), 33

10. J. Gordon Edwards, "Remembering Silent Spring and Its Consequences," Presentation for Doctors for Disaster Preparedness, Salt Lake City, Utah (August 3, 1996)

11. J. Gordon Edwards, "DDT Effects on Bird Abundance and Reproduction," in *Rational Readings on Environmental Concerns*, 199

12. Dixy Lee Ray and Lou Guzzo, *Trashing the Planet*, 72

13. J. Gordon Edwards, "DDT Effects on Bird Abundance and Reproduction," in *Rational Readings on Environmental Concerns*, 203

14. J. Gordon Edwards, "DDT Effects on Bird Abundance and Reproduction," in *Rational Readings on Environmental Concerns*, 204

15. J. Gordon Edwards, "DDT Effects on Bird Abundance and Reproduction," in *Rational Readings on Environmental Concerns*, 206

16. S. Milius, "Birds' eggs started to thin long before DDT," *Science News*, 153, (April 25, 1998), 261

17. J. Gordon Edwards, "DDT Effects on Bird Abundance and Reproduction," in *Rational Readings on Environmental Concerns*, 205

18. Edward Tenner, *Why Things Bite Back*, (New York, Alfred A. Knopf, 1996), 107

19. M. Alice Ottoboni, *The Dose Makes The Poison,* Second Edition, (New York, Van Nostrand Reinhold, 1997), 10

20. Melvin J. Grayson and Thomas R. Shephard, Jr., *The Disaster Lobby*, 34

21. J. Gordon Edwards, "Malaria: The Killer That Could Have Been Conquered," *21st Century*, 6, (Summer 1993), 29

22. J. Gordon Edwards, "Remembering Silent Spring and Its Consequences," Presentation for Doctors for Disaster Preparedness, Salt Lake City, Utah (August 3, 1996)

23. Adam J. Lieberman, "DDT, 1962" in *Facts Versus Fear*, (New York, American Council on Science and Health, September 1997), 4

24. Michael Fumento, "Truth Disruptors," *Forbes*, 162, (November 16, 1998), 146

25. Edward Tenner, *Why Things Bite Back*, 108

26. J. Gordon Edwards, "Remembering Silent Spring and Its Consequences," Presentation for Doctors for Disaster Preparedness, Salt Lake City, Utah (August 3, 1996)

27. Dixy Lee Ray and Lou Guzzo, *Trashing the Planet*, 70

28. J. Gordon Edwards, "Remembering Silent Spring and Its Consequences," Presentation for Doctors for Disaster Preparedness, Salt Lake City, Utah (August 3, 1996)

29. Gino J. Marco, Robert M. Hollingworth and William Durham, eds., *Silent Spring Revisited*, Washington, D.C., American Chemical Society, (1987), 193

30. B.E. Frazier, G. Chesters and G.B. Lee, "Pesticides in Soil," *Pesticides Monitoring Journal*, 4 (September 1970), 67

31. J.J. McKetta, "Don't Believe Everything You Read," in *Rational Readings on Environmental Concerns*, ed. Jay H. Lehr, (New York, Van Nostrand Reinhold, 1992), 350

32. J. Gordon Edwards, "DDT Effects on Bird Abundance and Reproduction," in *Rational Readings on Environmental Concerns*, 206

33. "Malaria Still Winning,", *Doctors for Disaster Preparedness Newsletter*, Volume XVII, No. 6, (November 2000)

34. J. Gordon Edwards, "Malaria: The Killer That Could Have Been Conquered," *21st Century*, 6, (Summer 1993), 21

35. J. Gordon Edwards, "Malaria: The Killer That Could Have Been Conquered," *21st Century*, 6, (Summer 1993), 22

36. Leonard T. Flynn, "The Birth of Environmentalism," in *Issues in the Environment*," ed. Kristine Napier, (New York, American Council on Science and Health, (June 1992), 14

37. Donald R. Roberts, et al., DDT Global Strategies and a Malaria Control Crisis in South America," *Emerging Infectious Diseases*, 3, (July-September, 1997), 295

Chapter 9

The Single Molecule Theory of Chemical Contamination

In 1990, Perrier bottled water was removed from the market because tests showed that samples contained 35 ppb (parts per billion) of benzene. Although this was an amount so small that only 15 years prior it would have been impossible to detect, it was assumed the product had to be withdrawn to protect public health.[1] This was, of course, science fiction fantasy. A person would have to consume 2.5 million bottles each week to approximate the intake of benzene (at the levels in the bottles) that had sickened rodents.[2]

This is an excellent example of the single molecule theory. This theory was the basis of the Delaney Clause to the Federal Food, Drug, and Cosmetic Act in 1958. It stated that no substance that has been shown to cause cancer in laboratory animals may be added to our food supply in any amount, no matter how small.[3] The word "added" applied to any synthetic chemicals, which at the time were assumed to account for up to 90% of cancers. Fortunately, the law did not apply the same standard to substances naturally present in food because if it did, we would most likely starve.

The single molecule theory is still around, and many folks subscribe to the theory that "one molecule" can cause cancer. Hopefully you will see this as preposterous after reading the rest of this chapter.

Thomas Jukes reports; "In the case of the 'single molecule theory' we should all be dead of cancer from the millions of molecules of arsenic, cadmium and chromium in each of our cells if the theory were valid. Each person has billions of molecules of carcinogens present naturally, including radioactive carbon and potassium, heavy metals, such as uranium (10,000 atoms per cell), steroid hormones, and numerous other carcinogens naturally present in foods."[4]

Table 9.1 lists some trace elements in the human body and their estimated quantities. Separately, the estimate for heavy metals in the human body ranges between ten thousand (10^4) and one hundred million (10^8) atoms per cell.

Table 9.1 – Trace Elements in the Human Body[a]

Element	Estimated Human Body Content
Arsenic	10 milligrams
Boron	48 milligrams
Cadmium	50 milligrams
Chromium	6 milligrams
Cobalt	1 milligram
Copper	70 milligrams
Fluorine	2.6 grams
Iron	4 grams
Iodine	20 milligrams
Lead	120 milligrams
Manganese	12 milligrams
Mercury	13 milligrams
Molybdenum	10 milligrams
Nickel	1 milligram
Selenium	10 milligrams
Silicon	18 grams
Tin	6 milligrams
Vanadium	100 micrograms
Zinc	2.3 grams

(a) John Lenihan, *The Crumbs of Creation*, (Bristol, Adam Hilger, 1988), 71

For discussion purposes, let's look at arsenic, cadmium and chromium, all of which are considered to be carcinogenic. According to Thomas Jukes, each human body contains approximately 4.4 mg, 30 mg and 6 mg respectively.[4] Jukes estimates for arsenic and cadmium are different from Lenihans' (see Table 1), while both agree on chromium. Regardless of which numbers are correct, Jukes' more conservative values still show the enormous amounts of these metals occuring naturally in the human body. Arsenic, cadmium and chromium would supply respectively 1×10^5 (100,000), 2×10^6 (2,000,000), and 0.7×10^6 (700,000) molecules per cell. Using 4.4 mg as the arsenic content of a normal, healthy human being, this translates into 9×10^{18} (a number far too large to put into words) molecules.[4] What does this all mean? Our own bodies go against the Delaney Clause.

Here's another example of big numbers. Alice Ottoboni discusses benzpyrene in her book, *The Dose Makes the Poison.* "Benzpyrene is a naturally occurring and relatively potent carcinogen that is virtually omnipresent in our environment as a product of the cooking or burning of any organic material. It has been determined that there are 50 micrograms of benzpyrene in about 2 lbs of charcoal broiled steak. A generous portion of steak would contain about 1/5th of a kg (7 oz). That portion of steak would contain about 10 micrograms benzpyrene. Ten micrograms is a very, very small quantity, as demonstrated by the fact that there are over 28 million micrograms in one ounce. But when one considers how many molecules are contained in 10 micrograms, that seemingly insignificant quantity takes on really formidable proportions. In 10 micrograms of benzpyrene there would be 24,000,000,000,000,000 molecules! To give this number a name, there would be about 24 quadrillion molecules of benzpyrene in a portion of charbroiled steak."[6]

Contaminants that now cause public indignation and regulatory panic, were not even detectable only 25 years ago. Analytical chemistry has improved enormously over the past few decades. Early on, we were detecting chemicals in water in the parts per thousand range. This is like finding one second in a 16 minute time span. Today we can measure contaminants in parts per quadrillion, which is equivalent to finding one second in a span of 32 million years![7] Or put another way, one part per quadrillion is one hair on the heads of all humans on earth[8] or, one golf ball compared to the size of the earth.[9]

Sidney Shindell suggests that we may ultimately get to counting molecules. When we do this, we automatically run into the law of diffusion. Shindell quotes scientist George Koelle: "If a pint of water is poured into the sea and allowed to mix completely with all the water on the surface of the earth, over 5,000 molecules of the original sample will be present in any pint taken subsequently. The general conclusion to be drawn from these calculations is that nothing is completely uncontaminated by anything else."[3]

At the smallest end of the spectrum, scientists at Oak Ridge National Laboratory detected a single atom of cesium in the presence of 10^{19} argon atoms and 10^{18} (that's quintillions) methane molecules.[10] Obviously, these days one can find just about anything with the ultra sensistive equipment that is available.

Let's go back to the Delaney Clause. Naturally occuring substances which fail the same animal cancer tests (i.e. that used in the Perrier incident) have been found in many foods. One example: about 99.99% of all pesticides in the human diet are natural pesticides from plants since they produce toxins to protect themselves against fungi, insects, and animal predators such as man.[11]

Fortunately, recent legislation has removed synthetic pesticide residues from any association with the Delaney clause, replacing the scientifically untenable "zero risk" requirement of Delaney with a stringent but attainable standard of "reasonable certainty of no harm."[12] Today, scientists believe that synthetic compounds cause only a small percentage of cancers. Easterbrook quotes Linda Fisher, former head of the EPA's toxic substances office: "Delaney became ridiculous. We were regulating extremely small amounts of synthetics in processed foods while having no controls for natural toxins in raw food, which research suggests is the greater problem. The situation made no sense."[13]

All of this, yet the thought behind the Delaney clause is still being used today by the media, politicians, and activists. Gregg Easterbook sums it up best: "The Delaney clause is a metaphor for the long standing political problem that alarms are more easily turned on than switched off.[13]

Each of us has billions of molecules of carcinogens present naturally in our bodies. So, of what practical value is it to learn that there is one part per trillion or one part per quadrillion of EDB or PCB, or whatever in our muffins, bottled water, or freshwater fish? All that is being shown is how good we are at analytical chemistry.

References

1. George G. Reisman, "The Toxicity of Environmentalism," in *Rational Readings on Environmental Concerns*," ed. Jay H. Lehr, (New York, Van Nostrand Reinhold, 1992), 819

2. Jeff Wheelwright, *Degrees of Disaster*, (New York, Simon & Schuster, 1994), 150

3. Sidney Shindell, "The Receding Zero," *ACSH News & Views*, (New York, American Council on Science and Health, Nov/Dec 1995)

4. Thomas A. Jukes, "Chasing a Receding Zero," in *Rational Readings on Environmental Concerns*," ed. Jay H. Lehr, (New York, Van Nostrand Reinhold, 1992), 332-333

5. John Lenihan, *The Crumbs of Creation*, (Bristol, Adam Hilger, 1988), 71

6. M. Alice Ottoboni, *The Dose Makes the Poison*, Second Edition, (New York, Van Nostrand Reinhold, 1997), 115

7. William H. Baarschers, *Eco-Facts & Eco-Fiction*, (London, Routledge, 1996), 146

8. Samuel R. Aldrich, *Smoke or Steam?*, (Winter Haven, Florida, Star Press, 1994), 73

9. Norman R. Ehmann, "Victims of Gnosophobia," *Journal of Environmental Health*, 53, (July/August 1990), 14

10. Mark S. Lesney, "Chain Reactions: Harvest of Silent Spring," *Today's Chemist*, 8 (March 1999), 83

11. Bruce N. Ames and Lois Swirsky Gold, "Environmental Pollution and Cancer: Some Misconceptions," in *Rational Readings on Environmental Concerns*," ed. Jay H. Lehr, (New York, Van Nostrand Reinhold, 1992), 153

12. "The Clause: The Beginning of the End," *Delaney Special Media Update*, (New York, American Council on Science and Health, September 1996)

13. Gregg Easterbrook, *A Moment on Earth*, (New York, Viking, 1995), 447

Chapter 10

Hormesis — Mother Knows Best

Did your mother ever tell you that a little bit of something is okay, but too much would make you sick? Mine did, but I forgot her advice as I was helping my uncle in his bakery. I was asked to clean five gallon cans of chocolate, and sampled too much of the chocolate left inside the cans. Of course, I became very sick, a case of too much of a good thing.

My mother was talking about hormesis, a scientific name that means low doses help you and high doses hurt (remember "the dose makes the poison?"). Hormesis applies throughout nature, with hundreds of studies describing experiments and observations supporting the beneficial effects of chemical and physical agents at low doses.[1]

"The word 'hormesis' derives from the same root as 'hormone,' from the Greek *hormo*, I excite," reports T.D. Luckey. Although the word is new, the concept is old, having been described by Hippocrates and others. All of them recognized that the dose is everything and stress is the common denominator. Small stresses stimulate, while excess stress inhibits.[2]

Hormology is the study of excitation. Examples from biochemistry include enzymes and their activation. Under proper conditions enzymes can increase reaction rates 1,000 times, but too much of the same material decreases the reaction rate. An interesting example is *tetrodotoxin*. This is a natural hallucinogen found in the puffer fish treasured for centuries in Japan. "A small amount of tetrodotoxin (which is more toxic than plutonium) produces euphoria; too much produces severe paralysis. In fact, overdoses kill dozens of Japanese each year. It is also the principle ingredient of the mixture used in creating zombies by Haiti witch doctors."[3] This is certainly an arcane, and weird, example but what follows are examples of chemicals you have certainly heard of, and how small doses have been found to be both helpful and necessary.

William Baarscher's notes: "Hormesis has been observed in bacteria, fungi and yeasts, plants, algae, invertebrates and vertebrates, and in cell cultures. The agents used in these studies include metals such as cadmium and lead, solvents, and many synthetic and natural chemicals. PCBs can promote the growth of juvenile Coho Salmon and minnows. The growth of clam and oyster larvae is promoted by low level concentrations of some 52 pesticides, and chlordane and lindane have been shown to promote the growth of crickets."[4]

Researchers have claimed chemically hormetic effects for crabs, clams, oysters, fish, insects, worms, mice, rats, ants, pigs, dogs, and humans. The range of agents employed in such studies has been wide, including numerous antibiotics, PCBs, ethanol, polycyclic aromatic hydrocarbons (PAHs), heavy metals, essential trace elements, pesticides, and a variety of miscellaneous agents, such as chemotherapeutic agents, solvents such as carbon tetrachloride, chloroform, cyanide, and sodium.[5]

The seafood industry of the lower Mississippi river thrives because of hormesis and low levels of what are considered "contaminants" have been proven to be critically important. Raphael Kazmann quotes Phillip West, Professor of Chemistry at Louisiana State University: "If the Mississippi River passing between Baton Rouge and New Orleans consisted of distilled water there would be no seafood industry such as we have now in Louisiana. Without copper contamination in the water, there would be no oysters. Traces of iron, manganese, cobalt, copper and zinc are essential for crabs, snapper, flounder, shrimp and other creatures that abound in Gulf waters.[6]

Another example of hormesis lives in the bottle of One A Day® you have in the medicine cabinet. Overdoses of the fat soluble vitamins such as A, E, and D are toxic.[7] Water soluble vitamin B6 can cause nerve damage at high doses, and hormones such as estrogen can cause cancer.[8] If you breathe pure oxygen at normal room pressure, you will suffer chest pain, coughing, and a sore throat within six hours. Hospitals have found that premature babies placed in incubators that were filled with oxygen enriched air went blind because of oxygen damage to their retinas.[9] Even water itself can be fatal if the rate of intake exceeds the body's capacity to process it (and I'm not talking about drowning). In Germany, a man died from cerebral edema and electrolyte disturbance because he drank 17 liters of water within a very short time.[10] Overuse of alcohol is associated with numerous organ toxicities, but these days you can read many claims about reduced risk of coronary heart disease, reduced mortality, etc. from moderate consumption of alcoholic beverages.

John Lenihan reports: "At the end of the 19th century, only two elements (iodine and iron) were known to be essential for human health. By 1935, only four more (copper, manganese, zinc and cobalt) had been added. But progress has been more rapid during the past 40 years, largely because the revolution in analytical chemistry has greatly enhanced the experimenter's capability to measure trace elements in the extremely small quantities present in plant and animal tissues and in food."[11] Here's a quick list of other elements now considered essential components in the human body: molybdenum, selenium, chromium, tin, vanadium, fluorine, silicon, nickel, arsenic, cadmium, and lead. The main reason essential trace elements are so extraordinarily potent is that they do most of their work as components of enzymes or hormones. Note that even lead and cadmium are included in the list (also note that the evidence is incomplete on these materials). Walter Heiby, in his tome *The Reverse Effect* (containing 1,216 pages and 4,821 references), lists many examples in which extremely minute amounts of these metals may be important to the human body.[12]

Practically every enzyme in the body has some small amount of metal involved in its chemical structure. As Wildavsky reports: "Zinc is used to maintain cell membranes and produce protein and energy; either too much or too little can lead to reduced growth; iron and molybdenum also must be kept at moderate levels."[8] Excess iron can lead to hemochromatosis, in which massive amounts of iron, in the form of hemosiderin, are laid down in the body tissues. Other cases of iron overload are specific anemias, where excessive breakdown of blood occurs and liver disease.[13] Copper is essential in minute quantities to the normal functioning of the human body. It makes possible the assimilation of iron, but its impact in large quantities has long been known to be toxic. Wilson's Disease is essentially chronic copper poisoning. Berton Roueche notes: "In it, the natural balance between copper ingestion and copper excretion is disturbed, and the copper thus retained in certain organs. The liver is its first and chief repository. In time, as the storage capacity of the liver is exhausted, the continuing accumulation of copper passes from the liver into the bloodstream and is carried to other organs for which copper has a grim affinity. These are most conspicuously the brain and the cornea of the eye." Symptoms of the disease include a sweeping range of neurological disturbances, but if diagnosed early enough it can be effectively treated with penicillamine, a derivative of penicillin.[14]

Chromium is not just for car and truck bumpers anymore. It has been claimed that chromium supplements offer promise as a new treatment for heart disease, high cholesterol and diabetes.[15] Selenium, once thought to be a poison and a carcinogen, is an antitumor agent in relatively low doses and an essential nutrient with a very small difference between recommended and harmful doses.[3] Arsenic compounds, which are known human carcinogens, have been shown to widely stimulate the growth of chickens, calves and pigs. Recently, arsenic trioxide was used successfully in intravenous form for the treatment of acute promyelocytic leukemia in humans.[16]

I am not trying to provide all inclusive information, and the claims in favor of these chemicals and minerals may change based on new research. But, that's really the point of all this. D.L. Stewart jokingly scoffs that every time one scientist announces that some food is bad for you, five other scientists release findings proving that it is bad for you only if you are a middle aged, 185 pound laboratory rat. He says scientists have issued so many contradictory reports about cholesterol that three years ago his wife gave up eating entirely.[17]

All kidding aside, there is enough evidence to prove that many chemicals and metals that are clearly toxic at certain levels offer benefits at low doses. The issue is that in most cases, we receive only the bad news. Toxicology studies almost exclusively focus on the dosage that kills. Research on most agents begins with the determination of LD_{50} values (the dose of a chemical that will kill 50 percent of the test animals).[5] In most studies, an animal consumes 50,000 to 100,000 times what a human would. Using the case of arsenic trioxide as an example, where research showed its effectiveness in treating a specific type of leukemia, shouldn't we be constantly looking for possible positive effects of these materials instead of only the high dosage environmental effects?

References

1. William H. Baarschers, *Eco-Facts & Eco-Fiction*, (London, Routledge, 1996), 71

2.   T.D. Luckey, *Radiation Hormesis*, (Boca Raton, CRC Press, 1991), 34

3.   T.D. Luckey, *Radiation Hormesis*, 37

4.   William H. Baarschers, *Eco-Facts & Eco-Fiction*, 72

5.   Edward J. Calabrese, Margaret E. McCarthy and Elaina Kenyon, "The Occurence of Chemically Induced Hormesis," *Health Physics*, 52, (1987), 531

6.   Raphael G. Kazmann, "Environmental Tyranny-A Threat to Democracy," in *Rational Readings on Environmental Concerns*, ed. Jay H. Lehr, (New York, Van Nostrand Reinhold, 1992), 311

7.   Elizabeth A. McKenna, "Hormesis: considerations and implications for human health risk assessment," *International Journal Environment and Pollution*, 9, (1998), 90

8.   Aaron Wildavsky, *Searching for Safety*, (New Brunswick, USA, Transactions Books, 1988), 153

9.   Ben Bova, *Immortality: How Science is Expandiing Your Lifespan and Changing the World*, (New York, Avon Books, 1998), 23

10. Dixy Lee Ray and Lou Guzzo, *Trashing the Planet*, (New York, Harper Perennial, 1992), 109

11. John Lenihan, *The Crumbs of Creation*, (Bristol, England, Adam Hilger, 1988), 46

12. Walter A. Heiby, *The Reverse Effect: How Vitamins and Minerals Promote Health and Cause Disease*, (Deerfield, Illinois, MediScience Publishers, 1988)

13. Len Mervyn, *Minerals and Your Health*, (New Canaan, Connecticut, Keats Publishing, 1984), 142

14. Berton Roueche, *The Medical Detectives*, (New York, Washington Square Press, 1982), 378

15. Len Mervyn, *Minerals and Your Health*, 107

16. Steven L. Soignet, et al., "Complete Remission After Treatment of Acute Promyeloctic Leukemia with Arsenic Trioxide," *New England Journal of Medicine*, 339, (1998), 1341

17. D.L. Stewart, "When It Comes to Science, Trust But Verify", *San Francisco Chronicle*, (April 15, 1998)

Chapter 11

A Vocabulary Lesson — Bioavailability and Chirality

Bioavailability and chirality are two words that should be in your vocabulary, if they aren't already. Both are attributes of chemicals, and unless you understand them, you cannot tell whether the amount of a chemical found through analysis is actually the amount available to do harm. In other words, tests currently used to detect some pollutants in soils may overestimate the risks they pose to living organisms. Let's take a look at both terms, as they are receiving increasing coverage in the technical literature.

Bioavailability when speaking of toxins, is the degree to which a toxin is available to harm organisms. There is considerable evidence that the properties of soil can greatly reduce a chemical's bioavailability. Cornell University researchers have reported that tests currently used to detect old DDT and other pollutants may overestimate the risk to living organisms. This means that the real issue for government regulators at toxic cleanup sites should be the "biological availability" of aging toxins. "Recent research has cast doubt on the validity of current analytical methods for assessing the risk from organic pollutants in soils," says Martin Alexander of Cornell, coauthor of a number of recent reports on bioavailability.[1]

What does this mean? Alexander further states, "Current methods determine the total concentration of compounds, not the amounts that are actually available to do harm. If we are not measuring bioavailability, we are overestimating, sometimes appreciably, the risk to biological organisms. Age can be an important factor because the compounds might be sequestered in the soil and are less likely to be absorbed by living organisms."[1]

Here are some experimental results on different compounds regarding bioavailability.

- Douglas Morrison and his colleagues report that as DDT, DDE, DDD, and dieldrin in field soils grow older, their bioavailability to earthworms declines sharply. Their findings indicate that more than from 50 to 85 percent of the pesticides were not in a form accessible to the test species.[2]

- Bioavailability varied greatly (a 28.2 percent to more than 99 percent decline) among six different soils for a variety of mutagens (chemicals that cause mutations). The chemicals included benzo(a)pyrene, 7,12-dimethylbenz(a)anthracene, 9-phenylanthracene, captain, and aldicarb.[3]

- Namhyun Chung and Martin Alexander confirmed that phenathrene and 4-nitrophenol are sequestered differently, and lose their bioavailability at different rates, depending on the soils in which they are found.[4]

- Many toxicants became less hazardous to test mammals within a short time after they are added to soil, whether the animals swallow them or absorb them through the skin. The include trichloroethylene, benzo(a)pyrene, 2,3,7,8-tetrachlorodibenzop-p-dioxin (TCDD), and m-xylene.[5]

- Lead is more or less bioavailable depending on its nature and form in contaminated soils and dusts. Researchers concluded that with present models from the EPA, we may be overestimating the bioavailability of lead from some environmental samples while underestimating it from others.[6]

- The presence of sandy clay and clay soil produced qualitative and quantitative differences in the manner in which benzene was available to the body of male rats following oral exposure.[7]

- Soil contaminated with dioxin from two manufacturing sites in New Jersey was unable to produce toxic effects in orally exposed guinea pigs, while similar amounts of pure dioxin did produce these effects.[8]

Summarizing on bioavailability, to figure out how badly living organisms have been exposed to a toxic chemical in soil, you need to know how much of that chemical is available to those species. Yet, today we measure danger not by the level that is biologically available, but rather by the total concentration of a chemical as determined by vigorous extraction. However, as Jixin Tang and his colleagues note: "Considerable evidence exists that the amount that is available to mammals, invertebrates, plants, and microorganisms is less, and sometimes appreciably less, than what you would expect from procedures based on vigorous extraction."[9] The organic compounds in Superfund and most other hazardous waste sites have been in contaminated soils for a long time. This very fact emphasizes the need for assessing the significance of aging to toxicity.[5]

Chirality is explained by John Casti in this way: "Everything in nature (except a vampire) has a mirror image, and all amino and nucleic acids come in both left-handed and right-handed forms. While these two forms are chemically identical in the sense of being formed from the same atomic constituents, the chemical actions of the two forms are quite different as a result of their 'twisting' in opposite directions." Casti also says this about chirality: "All like forms on Earth use exclusively left-handed amino acids to form proteins and right-handed nucleic acids to form the genetic material. As a consequence of this puzzling fact, we could starve to death on a planet where steaks were made out of right-handed proteins, since our body would be unable to break these proteins down to extract their energy."[10]

When chemical compounds exhibit chirality, the mirror image structures are called enantiomers.[11] One-fourth of all commercial pesticides are chiral and in some cases, the biological activity of a pesticide may be attributed to one enantiomer, while the enantiomer has little or no activity.[12] Rebecca Renner notes: "Half of the top best selling drugs, including barbiturates, Ritalin, and Ibuprofen are marketed as single enantiomers to avoid adverse side effects." She also points out that thalidomide illustrates how complex the chiral world can be. With this chiral drug, one enantiomer is beneficial and the other is highly toxic. Thalidomide, created in 1957 in Germany, was used as a sedative to help combat morning sickness in pregnant women; and caused birth defects. "The drug that caused the horrible birth in the 1960s contained both enantiomers. The bad enantiomer was responsible for the problems. Now there are proposals to remanufacture the beneficial enantiomer in pure form.[11]

A recent study in *Nature*[13] uncovered what Bonner Cohen calls "a hole in our knowledge of the chemicals we regulate that is so deep that what has passed for reliable data about them are flawed at best, and perhaps even entirely useless.[14] Much of the historical environmental data collected on pollutants is unreliable because so many of the chemicals are chiral, and the data do not distinguish which mirror images of certain chemicals were present and which were harmless. Cohen quotes David Lewis, coauthor of the *Nature* report: "The good news is that trace amounts of many of the environmental pollutants EPA is most worried about, including some DDT derivatives, PCBs and plasticizers, aren't as bad as previously thought. On the other hand, measures intended to protect the environment such as using treated sewage sludge as a fertilizer, will likely increase the persistence of the more toxic forms of some pesticides."[14]

Cohen further states: "The problems with pollutants is twofold: First, very few chemicals now considered major pollutants have been evaluated for their chirality at all, second environmental changes appear to alter which mirror images persist in the environment by affecting the soil microbes responsible for breaking down the chemicals." The *Nature* study further points out that the EPA has never considered the fact that many of the chemicals it regulates are chiral, with each individual form having completely different effects on living organisms. Since the EPA does not include chirality in its risk assessments, this raises a question about the validity of the agency's findings on, for example, pesticides, of which approximately one-fourth are chiral. "As the authors point out, current methods of determining which chemicals pose threats to the environment may be worthless in many cases.[14]

This work and others also demonstrate that significant environmental changes, such as tropical deforestation, may substantially affect how lone enantiomers of chiral pollutants persist in the environment, exacerbating the adverse effects of some while ameliorating the effects of others. As Lewis says: "It calls into question the accuracy and future relevance of current risk assessments for numerous pollutants, and underscores the need to better incorporate science in efforts aimed at protecting public health and the environment."[13, 15]

Bioavailability and chirality. Two terms and issues that continue to underscore the need for the EPA to let science (and not politics) guide their decisions.

References

1.   Roger Segelken, "Bioavailability is the Real Test for DDT Hazard," *Cornell University News Service*, (November 15, 1999)

2.   Douglas E. Morrison, Boakai K. Robertson, and Martin Alexander, "Bioavailability to Earthworms of Aged DDT, DDE, DDD, and Dieldrin in Soil," *Environmental Science & Technology*, 34, (2000), 709

3.   Renee R. Alexander and Martin Alexander, "Bioavailability of Genotoxic Compounds in Soils," *Environmental Science & Technology*, 34, (2000), 1589

4.   Namhyun Chung and Martin Alexander, "Differences in Sequestration and Bioavailability of Organic Compounds Aged in Dissimilar Soils," *Environmental Science & Technology*, 32, (1998), 855

5.   Martin Alexander, "How Toxic are Toxic Chemicals in Soil?", *Environmental Science and Technology*, 29, (1995), 2713

6.   D.P. Oliver, et al, "Measuring Pb Bioavailability from Household Dusts Using an In Vitro Model," *Environmental Science & Technology*, 33, (1999), 4434

7.   Rita M. Turkall, et al, "Soil Adsorption Alters Kinetic and Bioavailability of Benzene in Orally Exposed Male Rats," *Arch. Environ. Contam. Toxicol.*, 17 (1988), 159

8.   Thomas H. Umbreit, Elizabeth J. Hesse and Michael A. Gallo, "Bioavailability of Dioxin in Soil from a 2.4.5-T Manufacturing Site," *Science*, 232, (1986), 497

9.   Jixin Tang, Boakai K. Robertson and Martin Alexander, "Chemical-Extraction Methods to Estimate Bioavailability of DDT, DDE, and DDD in Soil," *Environmental Science & Technology*, 33 (1999), 4346

10.   J.L. Casti, *Paradigms Lost: Images of Man in the Mirror of Science*, (New York, William Morrow & Co., 1989), 85

11.   Rebecca Renner, "Researchers Point Toward Chiral Chemistry as Pollution Cure," *Environmental Science & Technology*, 34, (January 1, 2000), 9A

12. Markus D. Muller and Hans-Rudolf Buser, "Environmental Behavior of Acetamide Pesticide Stereoisomers. 2. Stereo- and Enantioselective Degradation in Sewage Sludge and Soil," *Environmental Science & Technology*, 29, (1995), 2031

13. David L. Lewis et al, "Influence of Environmental Changes on Degradation of Chiral Pollutants in Soils," *Nature* 401, (October 28, 1999), 898

14. Bonner Cohen, "Science Gap at the EPA," *Washington Times* (October 31, 1999)

15. David L. Lewis, "EPA Science: Casualty of Election Politics," *Nature*, 381, (June 27, 1996), 731

Chapter 12

Nature's Newly Discovered Chemical Behaves Like PCBs

Researchers with Canada's Wildlife Service have discovered an unusual brominated and chlorinated chemical, $C_{10}H_6N_2Br_4Cl_2$, (1,1-dimethyltetrabromodichloro-2,2-bipyrrole) in marine aquatics.[1] What is so unusual about this? Well, it behaves like PCBs (polychlorinated biphenyls), some of the most criticized industrial wastes. Yet, it differs from PCBs in one important way.

It is produced naturally by something in the oceans.

Environment Canada researchers have christened the chemical HDBPs for Halogenated Dimethyl BiPyrroles.[2] Tom Spears reports: "Characterization and speculation on how it originates have together cast doubt on a major premise used to damn DDT, PCBs, and other industrial chemicals; the premise that substances combining chlorine and organic 'carbonous' molecules (e.g. PCBs) do not result from biosynthesis and are therefore dangerous. Most environmentalists further contend that only unnatural toxicants build up in the tissues of animals that ingest food containing such chemicals."[3] Sheryl Tittlemier and her colleagues point out: "even though nearly 2,400 naturally produced organohalogens have been identified, natural sources are often ignored." They provide two examples: a report from the Science Advisory Board to the International Joint Commission on the Great Lakes which stated: "There is something non-biological about the halogenated organics," and articles in *Science* and elsewhere which contained the quote "some types of synthetic compounds, including halogenated hydrocarbons such as PCBs, are not found in nature."[1] Well, perhaps not so, as you have already read. Presently, it is not known if HDBPs are dangerous to humans or wildlife but their existence shows that some pollution laws depend at least partly on unreal distinction.[3]

One of the reasons chemicals like PCBs and DDT have been banned is because they are bioaccumulants, which according to Spears is "any contaminant of air, water, or food that builds up in living organisms because it is metabolized, or is eliminated, very slowly." He further points out that: "Some scientists claim that unnatural, or anthropogenic bioaccumulants cause reproductive problems in mammals, birds, and fish, a claim seriously questioned by many experts in this area. On the basis that chemicals combining chlorine and organic molecules are bioaccumulants, politicians in Canada, Mexico, and the United States have moved steadily toward 'zero-discharge' rules concerning them. Implicit in this is the basis that only unnatural chemicals are bioaccumulants."[3] However, HDBPs upset the apple cart since they are a PCB-like bioaccumulant in marine aquatics, and no longer can one assume that just because something is accumulating that it is man made. HDBPs have been found in Pacific and Atlantic Ocean samples, but not in samples from the Great Lakes. Since the Great Lakes is an industrial center inhabited by nearly 40 million people, if a chemical doesn't exist here, it probably is not industrial.[3]

Presently, no one knows where HDBPs originate. Wildlife researchers suspect that some organism secretes them as a defense against predators, perhaps marine bacteria or a slow macroscopic organism incapable of fighting, such as a sponge or a marine worm.[3] If these suspicions are correct, HDBPs are like the natural toxic chemicals that appear to be present in all plants protecting them against fungi, insects, and animal predators. Think about this for a moment. If you were a plant and could not run from predators or bite back, what would you do? If you wanted to survive, you might learn how to develop toxins to discourage predators. A lot of food we eat contains these natural toxins. Bruce Ames and his colleagues suggest that we are ingesting in our diet at least 10,000 times more, by weight, of natural pesticides than of manmade pesticide residues.[4]

Now, a few words about PCBs. There is no conclusive evidence that background PCB levels to which some occupational groups were exposed have resulted in acute effects, increased cancer risk, endocrine disruption, or widespread deterioration in children exposed to PCBs in utero. The only health effect that researchers have been able to attribute to PCBs were skin and eye irritation.[5] However, as William Baarschers points out, the general perception is the PCBs are "linked to cancer" or are "cancer causing chemicals." This has resulted in complex legislation that makes it difficult and expensive to transport PCBs or to clean up where they are present.[6]

Dr. Renate Kimbrough initially raised a flag in 1975 with her research that showed force-feeding rats their body weight in PCBs once a day (yes, an equal amount to their body weight each day) will eventually give some of them liver cancer. She has now completed a much larger study which followed more than 7,000 former General Electric employees who worked with PCBs between 1946 and 1977. Her results led to the conclusion that PCBs give no cause for concern.[7] This was the fifth such undertaking which concludes that PCBs pose no cancer risk to humans.[8] Government regulators might want to keep this in mind when they order PCB cleanup and disposal.

The EPA has ordered GE to spend $500 million dredging the Hudson River to remove PCBs which are embedded in the mud beneath the Hudson and are not generally dispersed in the water.[9] Explanations in the media about exactly what the EPA hopes to accomplish with half a billion dollars worth of dredging have been murky. All of this in spite of comments from the National Cancer Institute that they know of "no evidence" that eating fish (supposedly contaminated with PCBs) from the Hudson River poses a human health risk.[10] Please note in the references where the article occured in the Wall Street Journal, basically buried in the back of the paper.

As you have read, nature is producing a chemical which mimics PCBs in that it is considered bioaccumulative. You have also seen that the scientist that first condemned PCBs by force-feeding rats their own body weight in PCBs daily later concluded after much more testing that PCBs give no cause for concern. Even the National Cancer Society has said that fish contaminated with PCBs from the Hudson River pose no cancer risk.

C. Richard Cothern reports that our society generally accepts a risk ten times higher for a natural contaminant than that for a man-made contaminant.[11] Will this now apply with PCBs? Will we think differently about them since something that appears to act like them can be found in the oceans? Most of the public will not even hear about this recent finding. However, let someone spill PCBs or find some in a dump site in your city and you will hear about it on television or read it on the front page of the local paper. Here's a hypothetical scenario. What if future research shows that HDBPs are even more closely related to PCBs that we presently know? Who will the EPAs of the world charge with cleaning them from all the oceans? Will we ask Mother Nature to clean up her own problem, or perhaps God? Or, maybe folks will look at all the data on PCBs and conclude they really aren't a problem after all.

References

1. Sheryl A. Tittlemier, et al., "Identification of a Novel $C_{10}H_6N_2Br_4Cl_2$ Heterocyclic Compound in Seabird Eggs. A Bioaccumulating Marine Natural Product?" *Environmental Science & Technology*, 33, (1999), 26

2. Ross J. Norstrom, private communication with author, August 2, 2000

3. Tom Spears, "The Mystery of SNOB - Nature's PCB?", *Priorities for Health*, (New York, American Council on Science and Health, Volume 12, 2000), 10

4. Bruce N. Ames, Renae Magaw and Lois Swirsky Gold, "Ranking Possible Carcinogenic Hazards," *Science*, 236, (April 17, 1987), 271

5. "Position Paper of the American Council on Science and Health: Public Health Concerns About Environmental Polychlorinated Biphenyls (PCBs)", *Ecotoxicology and Environmental Safety*, 38, (1997), 71

6. William H. Baarschers, *Eco-Facts & Eco-Fiction*, (London, Routledge, 1996), 6

7. Renate D. Kimbrough, Martha L. Doemland and Maurice E. LeVois, "Mortality in Male and Female Capacitor Workers Exposed to Polychlorinated Biphenyls," in *Standard Handbook of Environmental Health, Science and Technology*," eds. Jay H. Lehr and Janet K. Lehr, (New York, McGraw-Hill, 2000), 15.73

8. B. McManus, "When Votes Outweigh the Facts," *New York Post*, (March 10, 1999)

9. William Tucker, "Junk Science, Green Gangsters & The Pursuit of PCBs," *The American Spectator*, 35, (January/February 2002), 53

10. Elizabeth M. Whelan, "Who Says PCBs Cause Cancer?," *Wall Street Journal*, (December 12, 2000), A26

11. C. Richard Cothern, "Introduction and Overview of Difficulties Encountered in Developing Comparative Rankings of Environmental Problems," in *Comparative Risk Assessment*, ed. C. Richard Cothern, (Boca Raton, Florida, Lewis Publishers, 1993), 7

Mother Nature — Do We Have The Power To Control Her Destiny?

Chapter 13

Nature, Frail or a Force to be Reckoned With?

When natural and man-made disasters crop up, we wring our hands and cry over the damaged area as if it is ruined forever. Nature has been cleaning itself since time began and has recovered from disasters far more serious than anything man has fashioned. Whether it is oil spills, volcanic eruptions, wars, nuclear holocausts, or toxic wastes, nature has effective cleaning and adaptation mechanisms that have gone unreported.

Oil spills provide an excellent example of nature's resiliency. The damage from even a horrendous spill of crude is relatively modest, and as far as can be determined, of relatively short nature. [1] The Exxon Valdez spilled 11 million gallons of crude into Prince William Sound in 1989. Within just three years the sound was so close to its "pre-spill" state that navigation charts had to be used to determine that the spill actually occurred. Some research shows the cleanup actually did more damage than the spill. [2]

Under public pressure, Exxon and the Coast Guard put together a cleanup that was so massive in scale that at its peak it produced the greatest concentration of vessels engaged in a single operation since the Normandy landing in World War II. In many locations high pressure hot water was used to blast away oil. This killed the microbial life that moors the food chain. By contrast, beaches that were left alone for experimental purpose cleaned themselves via wave action, microbic digestion and other factors, thus keeping the microbial anchor alive and keeping the food chain intact.

These are the traditional defenses that nature has prepared against petroleum. After all, petroleum is a naturally occurring product which continually "spills" from the Earth's crust. Research conducted by the

National Academy of Sciences found that offshore drilling accounts for less than two percent of the oil in the worlds' oceans, with the balance coming from natural seepage. Since petroleum enters the biosphere on a natural basis, some organisms have adapted to metabolize it.[3] Scientists from Texas A&M University have discovered thriving communities of mussels and tube worms feeding on natural gas and oil seeps on the floor of the Gulf of Mexico, more proof that oil is a natural part of the marine ecosystem.[4]

Another disaster and natural recovery example is the Amoco Cadiz which ran aground off the coast of France in 1978 and spilled six times as much as the Exxon Valdez. No long term effect on the bird population has been discovered in that area. Where no attempt was made to remove the oil, natural processes restored marshes within five years. In areas that were cleaned, restoration took seven to eight years.[5]

Why do we rush to clean up these spills? One clear reason is response to media pressure. Only the most hardened soul cannot respond sympathetically to pictures of oil soaked birds either dead or dying. In the heat of the moment, few ask how nature will clean this wound. Rather, most of us blame those who created the spill and clamor to quickly fix the problem, even though in many cases nature can do a much better job than we humans.

Toxic waste generated by industry is constantly under attack, which is understandable because we need to ensure that large amounts of toxins are not dumped into the environment. However, in the following example, you will see that nature can adapt to even the worst situation.

Foundry Cove is on the Hudson River across from West Point. It has an impressive manufacturing history. During the Revolutionary War, a forge at the cove produced chains that were stretched across the Hudson to slow down British warships. Ammunition was produced in Foundry Cove during the Civil War, and then the manufacture of batteries began 50 years ago.

Beginning around 1953, industry in the area dumped more than 100 tons of nickel-cadmium waste into the cove and nearby river.[6] Arsenic, lead and other toxins were also dumped into the river.[7] This dumping was halted in the late 1970s due to the excellent efforts of local citizens.

Jeffrey Levinton found that as much as 25% of the cove's bottom sediment consisted of cadmium, which is highly toxic. Yet, many bottom dwelling invertebrates were present in numbers no fewer than in unpolluted areas at other sites. In an effort to learn why, Levinton investigated the cadmium tolerance of the most common invertebrate in the cove, a relative of the earthworm with the difficult to remember and pronounce name *Limnodrilus hoffmeisteri*. Whereas local cove worms thrived and reproduced, *Limnodrilus* from a nearby region showed clear signs of distress or died when placed in Foundry Cove. Offspring of Foundry Cove worms raised in clean muds were also tolerant of cadmium, leading to the conclusion that genes were largely responsible for the tolerance. This degree of metal tolerance could have evolved in just 2-4 generations, or a couple of years. This was verified by exposing worms from an unpolluted site to cadmium laden sediment and breeding the survivors. By the third generation, the descendants had 2/3 of the cadmium tolerance found in the Foundry Cove worms.[6]

Levinton states that this capacity for rapid adaption in the face of novel environmental challenge was startling, since no population of worms in nature have ever faced conditions like the one humankind created in Foundry Cove. Furthermore, although some species inhabiting nearby waterways are missing from Foundry Cove, most adapted to the unusual conditions. Just 100 yards downstream is an Audubon Society sanctuary for migrating birds, which has prospered.[6]

On the morning of May 18, 1980 the top of Mount St. Helens "rocketed into the stratosphere." The mountain had shook and bulged for weeks before suddenly losing 1,300 feet of its top in a landslide and explosion that, according to the U.S. Forest Service, sent a cloud 15 miles up, knocked over 96,000 acres of trees, spread 540 million tons of ash over three states and killed 57 people. It was the largest landslide in recorded history. Spirit Lake, near the base of Mount St. Helens was filled with ash and tree trunks raising its bottom 200 feet.

Scientists believed it would take at least a decade before the area would support a wide variety of life again. Yet, as Jim McCausland reports, "Within three years 90% of the plants and animals that have lived in the pre-eruption blast zone had regained at least a toehold there; within 15 years wild trout were swimming in Spirit Lake."[8]

Let's take a look at the ravages of war on the environment. In 1942 the earth around Stalingrad was scorched by retreating Russian troops, yet became a living forest anew within a decade without any help from the Moscow regime. During the Korean War agricultural areas were continuously bombed. However, within a few years these areas showed no ill effect of long-term damage. In more recent times the United States dropped 19 million gallons of herbicides, including 11 million gallons of Agent Orange on the jungles of Vietnam. Today, these jungles are as lush as before the war, again without our assistance. In 1992 researchers near the Vietnam-Laos border found the first new large mammal species detected on the earth in 50 years, a cow-goat named the Vu-Quang ox. Two years later they found a second new large species, the giant muntjac deer. As Easterbrook points out "These creatures have been evolving, and surviving in a jungle just 20 miles from the Ho Chi Minh Trail — the most intensely bombed target in military history."[9]

Nature has also demonstrated the capacity for natural recovery from an atomic holocaust. T.D. Luckey demonstrates the remarkable survival of a rat colony on Enjebi Island in the Eniwetok atoll. Enjebi is part of the Marshall Islands and site of the "X-ray Nuclear Test" in 1948 during Operation Sandstone. "Within one year following four nuclear explosions, healthy rats emerged from the protection of cable tunnels. Pregnancy rates, sex ratios, and average numbers of embryos per litter were comparable with those found before the four nuclear devastations. The colony rapidly expanded to fill the 250 acre island. No mutations were observed."[10]

Guy Murchie reports that in 1964, scientists studied the remains of Namu, a coral isle of the Bikini atoll whose entire top had been blown off by a hydrogen bomb in 1956. "They found it covered with sedge, beach magnolia, morning glory vines and the white blossomed messerschmidia tree, with many kinds of birds flying gaily about, singing and raising their young, insects buzzing and burrowing, and fish swarming in the lagoons."[11]

A couple more examples hopefully continue to make the argument.

Peter LaGoy reports, "Many of the streams in Colorado down gradient from mining sites contain heavy metals at levels well above national water quality criteria, but apparently nobody has bothered to tell the fish they should be dead."[12]

Deer mice from areas of Los Angeles with high ambient air pollution are significantly more resistant to ozone than are mice from areas with low ambient pollution (56% versus 5% survival). Laboratory-born progeny of these mice show similar response patterns, indicating that the resistance is genetically based.[13]

Dixy Lee Ray discusses a colony of rats that occupy a mound in the Brazilian area of Morro do Ferro. This is a weathered mound, 250 meters tall that contains an estimated 30,000 metric tons of thorium and 100,000 tons of rare earths. The radiation level is so high that autoradiographs (photographs produced by radiation) show plants on the mound actually glowing in the dark. Rats breathe an atmosphere containing radon levels at up to 100 pCi (picocurie) per milliliter. The overall radiation doses they receive are roughly three times the concentration that should produce tumors or other radiation effects. Yet, no abnormalities were found on 14 rats that were trapped and autopsied.[14]

We give immense credit to the natural powers of destruction, such as lightning, tornadoes, hurricanes, floods and earthquakes. We are shown time and time again that nature is a force to be reckoned with. Yet, we also consider nature to be amazingly frail and unable to heal wounds either self-inflicted or inflicted by man. As seen, nature has an amazing ability to heal itself and adapt to situations we would think are unbearable. In some situations we rush to clean up our messes, which is understandable, but we need to realize that in many cases nature will do a much better job alone.

References

1. Jeff Wheelright, *Degrees of Disaster*, (New York, Simon & Schuster, 1996), 133

2. Gregg Easterbrook, *A Moment on Earth*, (New York, Viking, 1995), 55

3. Gregg Easterbrook, *A Moment on Earth*, 56

4. Joseph L. Bast, Peter J. Hill and Richard C. Rue, *Eco-Sanity*, (Lanham, Maryland, Madison Books, 1994), 150

5. P.J. O'Rourke, *All The Trouble in the World*, (New York, Atlantic Monthly Press, 1994), 160

6. Jeffrey S. Levinton, "The Big Bang of Animal Evolution," *Scientific American*, 267 (November 1982), 84

7. Gregg Easterbrook, *A Moment on Earth*, 59

8. Jim McCausland, "St. Helens springs to life," *Sunset*, (May, 1997), 24

9. Gregg Easterbrook, *A Moment on Earth*, 60

10. T.D. Luckey, *Radiation Hormesis*, (Boca Ration, CRC Press, 1991), 65

11. Guy Murchie, *The Seven Mysteries of Life*, (Boston, Houghton Mifflin Company, 1978), 388

12. Peter K. LaGoy, *Risk Assessment: Principles and Applications for Hazardous Waste and Related Sites*, (Park Ridge, New Jersey, Noyes Publications, 1994), 167

13. Kathleen E. Richkind and Allen D. Hacker, "Responses of Natural Wildlife Population to Air Pollution," *Toxicology and Environmental Health*, 6 (1980), 1

14. Dixy Lee Ray, "Radiation Around Us," in *Rational Readings on Environmental Concerns*, ed. Jay H. Lehr, (New York, Van Nostrand Reinhold, 1992), 594

Chapter 14

Species Extinction May Not Be Caused by Pollution

Are we spending too much time blaming pollution and therefore not finding the real reasons behind declines in wild animal populations? Isn't blaming pollution the easy way out of perhaps a much more complex reason, or are we ignoring a simple answer because it is not dynamic or sinister enough?

"Biologists usually blame pollution and predation for species extinction, but the real culprits may be humans spreading disease," noted Debora MacKenzie in a recent issue of New Scientist. Her article quotes Andy Dobson of Princeton University: "Forgetting disease was a big omission in our thinking about wild populations."[1]

Jane Orient writes about studies on people: "In the furor over volatile organic compounds, pesticides and other chemicals, we tend to forget that infectious diseases are in fact the leading killer of human beings worldwide. In the United States, more than 740 million infectious disease events occur every year, resulting in 200,000 deaths and more than $17 billion in direct care."[2] It should not be surprising that wild animals may have a similar problem. Perhaps if we spent more time and resources studying infectious diseases in animals, rather than blaming pollution, we would find some relief. What follows are several examples of studies that have linked infectious disease to species decline instead of the common belief pollution was the culprit.

Hannah Holmes in her fascinating book, *The Secret Life of Dust*, reports the following. "A dust related disease, not pollution, stands charged with slaying purple sea fan corals. Dust from the Sahara has long beaten a path across the Atlantic Ocean to rain down on the Car-

ibbean. But in the 1970s a terrible drought in the African Sahel region south of the great desert began to send extra dust rolling down
this skyway, and as the falling dust grew thick in the Caribbean in the
early 1980s, scientists saw a plague sweep through the coral reefs.
Coincident with the dust invasion, two species were nearly wiped out,
a species of sea urchin was decimated, and the purple sea fans developed dark, lumpy lesions. It took some sleuthing but a scientist has
pinned the sea-fan plague on a fungus in the Saharan dust."[3]

I think most of you will remember the recent concerns about frogs
and other amphibians that were missing limbs, and this tragedy being
tied by some scientists to the hole in the ozone layer over the Antarctic. Researchers have now established that the deformities are due to a
naturally occurring parasite.[4] Peter Daszak, a wildlife disease specialist at the University of Georgia at Athens who helped identify the
fungal plague that is killing off the world's amphibians says, "When
there is a sudden die-off of wild animals, people usually suspect pollution." An enormous amount of time has been spent pursuing environmental explanations for amphibian deaths, when disease was the
primary cause for the mass mortality.[1]

A type of land snail that scientists were trying to pull back from the
brink of extinction in a captive-breeding program provides the first
documented case of an infection wiping out the last remnants of an
entire species. Dan Ferber reports that a parasite had infected the
snails' digestive glands.[5] Experts say the finding points out the urgent
need to guard against infectious disease when nursing species.

Scientists have undertaken far fewer studies on how pathogens affect wildlife than have been done with humans. Peter Daszak sums it
up concisely: "There are few regulations concerning exotic disease
threats to wild animals, and few systems for surveillance are in place.
Current measures for the detection and control of human and livestock emerging infectious diseases are inadequate for the identification of similar threats to wildlife.[6]

Although some ecologists and wildlife biologists are beginning to
accept that pathogens can cause extinctions, few were prepared for some
of the many, apparently innocuous forms a disease reservoir can take.
"Burgeoning livestock populations and even pet animals are creating a

multitude of artificial reservoirs. Domestic ducks harbor duck plague, a herpes virus that causes massive die-offs in wild ducks. African village dogs spread distemper and rabies to lions and wild canids.[1] In 1994, one thousand lions, 1/3 of the population in Tanzania's Serengeti National Park, died from canine distemper, a disease they were not supposed to get.[7] Feeding birds in your garden can contribute to the problem since the bird table provides a mixing bowl for droppings and food, as birds congregate in numbers and combinations that would never occur in the wild. "The picturesque bird tables may be behind the worsening epidemics of salmonella and E. coli that have killed thousands of songbirds, especially finches, in Europe and North America in recent years."[1]

Stephanie Pain says that one of the reasons wild animals are so vulnerable to the diseases of domestic animals is simply because they have not been exposed to them before. These pathogens attack wild populations as common European diseases such as measles, flu and smallpox decimated the Native Americans after the Spanish conquest. Some degree of immunity evolves over long association with a virus or other agent of disease. But, a population that has never encountered the disease before has no defense at all.[7]

Why are these diseases wreaking havoc on wildlife now? One reason is that like humans, animals do a lot more traveling these days. Peter Daszak suggests that techniques for transporting animals must be improved.[1] Animals that are reintroduced into the wild should be checked for infection and any deaths investigated. Also, people who work with animals may be causing the problem. For example, Ian Anderson suggests that the frog-killing fungus that turned up at about the same time in Panama, Australia, and the United States may be spreading because of the very herpetologists who spend their lives studying endangered amphibians.[8]

I guess headlines that read "Frogs Missing Legs Because They Have Bugs" just would not sell papers, or get people to watch cable news. Furthermore, it seems that perhaps the desire to blame pollution, a much more sinister culprit, has taken the focus off the real threat to animal species, infectious disease. Have we spent too much time taking the easy way out, and perhaps lost more than we would have?

References

1. Debora MacKenzie, "Sick to Death", *New Scientist*, 167, (August 5, 2000), 32

2. Jane M. Orient, "Microorganisms, Molecules, and Environmental Risk Assessment: Assumptions and Outcomes," in *Standard Handbook of Environmental Science, Health and Technology*, eds. Jay H. Lehr and Janet K. Lehr, (New York, McGraw-Hill, 2000), 12.53

3. Hannah Holmes, *The Secret Life of Dust*, (New York, John Wiley & Sons, 2001), 91

4. S. Fred Singer, "Mastering the problem of environmental quality," *Environment and Climate News*, 14, (February 2001), 4

5. Dan Ferber, "Bug Vanquishes Species," *Science*, 282, (October 9, 1998), 215

6. Peter Daszak, Andrew Cunningham, and Alex H. Hyatt, "Emerging Infectious Diseases of Wildlife - Threats to Biodiversity and Human Health," *Science*, 287 (January 21, 2000), 443

7. Stephanie Pain, "Plague Dogs," *New Scientist*, 154, (April 19, 1997), 32

8. Ian Anderson, "A Great Leap Forward," *New Scientist*, 158, (June 27, 1998), 4

Chapter 15

Killer Rocks: Please Spend My Money Here!

As we conclude this section on pollution, let me ask you a question. If you were Mother Earth, which would worry you more, killer rocks that can destroy the biosphere of entire continents, or parts per quadrillion of toxins that might cause a few additional cancer deaths per decade?

If we could ask nature how it might rank environmental calamities that have occurred so far, all leading contenders would be natural, not man-made. Gregg Easterbrook says this: "The biosphere that some environmentalists today contend cannot resist so much as an oil spill or an overzealous crew of loggers, has in the past survived the unimaginable multiple whammy of the atmosphere set on fire by a killer rock strike; followed by years of summer frost, megasmog, and acid rain from hell; followed by decades or centuries of continuous global volcanism set loose by the rock's effect on the crust. This point is not made to rationalize oil spills or clear cutting. No human environmental misuse should ever be justified on the grounds that the environment can recover, even if that is true. The point here is simply to compare the sorts of people-caused environmental insults that men and women today reflexively describe as "disasters" against the genuine disasters nature has survived in the past."[1]

There have been five massive extinctions of life on Earth, with the most recent occurring about 65 million years ago. An object about 10 kilometers across impacted Earth, ending the Cretaceous period and wiping out the dinosaurs. The energy released was equivalent to the explosion of about 100 million megatons of TNT, which is about 10,000 times the energy of the simultaneous explosion of all the nuclear weapons on earth in the 1980s before the superpowers started to dismantle their stockpiles.[2]

Astronomers report that Earth has been bombarded by asteroids and comets large enough to cause global environmental catastrophe about once every 300,000 years. This suggests that our "fragile" environment has taken some serious beatings over its lifetime, and has always managed to come back. From 1975 to 1992 military satellites detected 136 large explosions caused by asteroids or comets in the upper atmosphere, an average of 8 per year. The typical force of the explosion was 15 kilotons, about the same as Little Boy, the atomic bomb dropped on Hiroshima. Since the satellites only see about 1/10 of the Earth at any moment, it is projected that the true rate of upper atmosphere strikes may be more than 80 per year.[3] John and Mary Gribbin estimate "that 2,000 asteroids, each more than a kilometer across, are in Earth's crossing orbits, accompanied by a million objects between 100 meters and 1 kilometer across, and at least 500 million smaller objects (down to 10 meters across)."[4]

The idea of an asteroid or comet hitting the earth is not farfetched. In 1908, in a remote area of Siberia called Tunguska, a vast fireball exploded with the force of 15,000 kilotons. The heat incinerated vast herds of reindeer and charred tens of thousands of evergreens across hundreds of square miles.[5] The area is so remote that few humans died. However, if the Tunguska rock had arrived a few hours later when the Earth had turned a little more, St. Petersburg would have been destroyed along with most of its inhabitants. This would have changed the course of history since one of the residents was a person named Vladimir Ilich Ulyanov, also known as Lenin.[6] Smaller chunks have reached the ill-fated town of Wethersfield, Connecticut twice. In April of 1971 a meteorite caused minor damage to a house in this town, and another damaged a second house less than a kilometer away on November 8, 1982.[7]

In 1989 a 1,000 meter asteroid was discovered only after it had crossed the Earth's orbit at a spot where we had been a scant six hours before. In May 1996, another asteroid about the same size was discovered only four days before it sped across Earth's orbit, ultimately missing us by only four hours.[8]

The risk of death from an asteroid impact is in the same range of probability as the risk of death from a hurricane or airplane crash. Why? Even though asteroid impacts are unlikely in any given year, when they do occur they have the potential to generate enormous destruction.[9] Clark Chapman and David Morrison say that the chances of a typical U.S. citizen's death from a killer rock from space is much higher than the widely publicized threats from certain carcinogens, poisoning by commercial foods and pills that have been tampered with, and fireworks accidents.[10]

So, let's compare some numbers here.

Average risk of death of an individual over a 50 year period, as estimated from historical frequencies and current populations

WORLDWIDE:	Risk of death from[a]	
	Asteroid impact	1 in 20,000
	Volcanic eruption	1 in 30,000
U.S. Only	Risk of death from	
	Auto accident	1 in 100
	Electrocution	1 in 5,000
	Airplane crash	1 in 20,000
	Hurricane	1 in 25,000
	Tornado	1 in 50,000
	Lightning	1 in 130,000
	Earthquake	1 in 200,000
	Fireworks accident	1 in 1 million[b]
	Botulism (food poisoning)	1 in 3 million[b]
	Drinking water with EPA limit of trichloroethylene	1 in 10 million[b]

a. Ernest Zebrowski, Jr., *Perils of A Restless Planet*, 221
b. Clark R. Chapman and David Morrison, "Impacts on Earth by asteroids and comets: assessing the hazard," *Nature*, 367, (January 6, 1994), 33

Here are a few more numbers for you to consider. We spend billions of dollars on programs in which we worry about infinitesimal amounts of substances in our environment whether they can be proven dangerous or not. For example, one estimate puts the cost of avoiding one case of cancer through Superfund cleanup at $11.7 billion[11], while another says it exceeds $15 billion.[12] Take your pick, either is an enormous number. Some of this zeal is an attempt to save lives in future generations. However, as Bernard Cohen has pointed out: "The lives saved are those of people living many thousands of years in the future, who bear no closer relationship to us than those now living in under developed countries whose lives we disdain to save at one millionth of these costs (see Chapter 17: The Cost of a Life and Interventions later in this book). In the second place, there is an excellent chance that a cure for cancer will be found in the next few thousand years, in which case these deaths will never materialize and the money will be wasted."[13]

Can you imagine spending anywhere from \$11-15 billion on avoiding one case of cancer? In comparison, we are doing little, if nothing to identify potential threats from outer space in the form of killer rocks. A NASA workshop in 1992 resulted in a proposal called the Spaceguard Survey, which consisted of a scheme to monitor near-Earth space hazards using a specially built network of telescopes. The startup cost would be about \$50 million and running costs of around \$10 million per year. Over a period of 20 to 30 years Spaceguard could identify all the potentially dangerous asteroids in the inner solar system and give a few months warning of the arrival of a threatening comet.[14] But where are we on this program? David Morrison points out that at present, the number of people in the world who are searching for NEOs (near earth objects) are about the same number as required to run two McDonald's.[15]

I for one would like to see a few of these millions and billions of dollars we are throwing at hypothetical contaminants spent instead looking for killer rocks from space. Future generations might well find a cure for cancer and heart disease, but will not be able to prevent outer space from throwing rocks the size of mountains at us. Although it may not be tomorrow or next year or in a thousand years, it will happen again and the right thing to do is to start preparations right now. Can we avoid asteroids hitting us? I don't know. I would like to think that the images shown in the movie Armageddon are attainable, but perhaps it is unavoidable. Whatever the chances, I would think we should at least look deeper into the subject. Steven Milloy says it best in his review of a Washington Post article that discussed global warming and killer rocks from space: "Pardon me, but if we are going to be concerned about doomsday scenarios, I would be more concerned about getting clocked by space rubble."[16]

Even after all this, if the doomsday scenario still seems a bit far-fetched, Eugenie Samuel recently reported on an international workshop of experts on the asteroid threat. One conclusion: "There is now an estimated 1 in 5 chance that an asteroid big enough to destroy a city will hit the Earth in the next 100 years."[17] If you want to worry about the future generations, better start now.

References

1. Gregg Easterbrook, *A Moment on Earth*, (New York, Viking, 1995), 33

2. John Gribbin and Mary Gribbin, *Fire on Earth: Doomsday, Dinosaurs, and Humankind*, (New York, St. Martin's Press, 1996), 9 and 29

3. Gregg Easterbrook, *A Moment on Earth*, (New York, Viking, 1995), 29

4. John Gribbin and Mary Gribbin, *Fire on Earth: Doomsday, Dinosaurs, and Humankind*, 228

5. John Gribbin and Mary Gribbin, *Fire on Earth: Doomsday, Dinosaurs, and Humankind*, 45

6. John Gribbin and Mary Gribbin, *Fire on Earth: Doomsday, Dinosaurs, and Humankind*, 50

7. Bob Berman, "Struck by a Meteor." *Discover*, 12 (August 1991), 28

8. Ernest Zebrowski, Jr., *Perils of A Restless Planet*, (Cambridge, United Kingdom, Cambridge University Press, 1997), 217

9. Ernest Zebrowski, Jr., *Perils of A Restless Planet*, 220

10. Clark R. Chapman and David Morrison, "Impacts on Earth by asteroids and comets: assessing the hazard," *Nature*, 367, (January 6, 1994), 33

11. D. Mastio, "Reform Speeds Toxic Cleanups," *The Detroit News* (2000), May 9

12. Philip H. Abelson, "Remediation of Hazardous Waste Sites," *Science*, 255, (February 21, 1992), 901

13. Bernard L. Cohen, "Perspectives on the Cost Effectiveness of Life Saving," in *Rational Readings on Environmental Concerns*, ed. Jay H. Lehr, (New York, Van Nostrand Reinhold, 1992), 466

14. John Gribbin and Mary Gribbin, *Fire on Earth: Doomsday, Dinosaurs, and Humankind*, 233

15. David Morrison, private communication, October, 22, 2002

16. Steven J. Milloy, comments on an article in the *Washington Post*, February 16, 1997, junkscience.com/news/asteroid.html

17. Eugenie Samuel, "Asteroid threat is greater than ever," *New Scientist*, 175, September 14, 2002, 6

Assessing Risks and the Costs of Life

Chapter 16

The Precautionary Principle — Better Off Staying in Bed

Better safe than sorry.

Just in case.

Above all, do no harm.

Do nothing new until it has been absolutely proven to be completely safe.

All of the above have been used to describe the **precautionary principle**. Few policies for risk management have created as much controversy as the precautionary principle which emerged in Europe in the 1970s and is now incorporated into environmental statutes and policies worldwide. Among these are the margin of safety requirement for setting ambient air quality standards under the Clean Air Act, the Rio Declaration from the 1992 Earth Summit, and industrial practices for product testing and environmental management.[1]

Despite its seemingly widespread political support, the precautionary principle has caused endless controversy, in part because of confusion surrounding its interpretation. One legal analysis identified 14 different formulations of the principle in treaties and nontreaty declarations. The "strongest" formulation of the principle calls for absolute proof of safety before new technologies may be adopted. The World Charter for Nature (1982) states that "where potential adverse effects are not fully understood, the activities should not proceed." Kenneth Foster et al., point out that if this were interpreted literally, no new technology could meet this requirement. Some less stringent formulations open the door to cost-benefit analysis and discretionary judgment, but others call for decisions in the absence of any scientific evidence.[2]

If we followed the stronger precautionary principles, something as common as salt, pepper, sugar, or Vitamin D could never be added to prepared foods, for fear they might one day be proven carcinogens. The last three have been shown to cause cancer in at least one animal test.[3]

If the precautionary principle was used decades ago for polio vaccines and antibiotics, it certainly may have prevented some harm and even death by delaying or denying approval of those products based on their possible side effects. However, that precaution would have come *at the expense of millions of lives lost* to infectious diseases.[4]

The precautionary principle is about risk, and sorry to say it, but life is a risk. If you want to advocate this principle in your daily living, perhaps you should not even get out of bed in the morning. When you get out of bed, you are taking a risk, because about 20 Britons die every year as a result of falling out of bed, while 30 die in their bath. Around 600 die on their own stairs.[5] Even your clothes can try to kill you. In 1997, emergency room doctors saw some 50,000 patients who had suffered "clothes-calls." A pair of socks can create a singular disaster. Hundreds of people are treated annually for slipping and falling while trying to put on their socks.[6] Risk and living are inseparable. Hospitals make people sick, exercise can hurt you, herbal tea is laced with carcinogens. Even breathing can kill, according to a prominent theory that cancer is caused by oxygen radicals created through the burning of fat.[7]

We could go on and on with examples. If you really want to capture the spirit of these fearful times, I suggest Melinda Muse's book, *I'm Afraid, You're Afraid; 448 Things to Fear and Why*. This A to Z compilation will show you there is nowhere to run, nowhere to hide. It's a must read if you are a worry wort.

Let's get back to the precautionary principle and its advocates. Terry Yosie reports the following: "In recent years advocates of the precautionary principle have sought to narrow both the information and the choices available for society to make important decisions, ranging from public policy issues to consumer products and the application of science. Historically, the use of a narrowly focused precautionary principle has resulted in some devastating consequences. For example, since 1991 an ongoing cholera epidemic has caused 1.3 million illnesses and approximately 12,000 deaths throughout Latin America.

A principal cause of this epidemic has been the misconception that disinfection by-products pose a greater health risk to public health than pathogens. Latin American governments succumbed to pressures from precautionary principle advocates and stopped the chlorination of drinking water supplies."[1]

This very issue, the use of chlorine in drinking water, is rearing its head in the United States right now, as activists are pushing federal legislation to ban its use. Anti-chemical groups have been asserting that higher breast cancer rates in Long Island are due to chlorine in the water supply (and exposure to other chemicals) and lobbied hard for funding of a study by the National Cancer Institute. The results of the study showed no link between cancer rates and the scapegoated chemicals, and even completely exonerated chemicals as a cause of the area's elevated cancer rate. Even though they could not win in the laboratory, anti-chemical groups are using the precautionary principle to push politicians so that they might prevail in the U.S. Senate. Senate Bill 1602 would force facilities to replace chlorine and other chemicals with "inherently safer technology." If this happens, politics will trump science, ignoring completely what has happened in Latin America, and ignoring not only the National Cancer Institute test, but also tests from the *New England Journal of Medicine* and the Harvard Center for Cancer Prevention.[8] Can you imagine cholera coming to America, or the massive numbers of bacterial infections? These activists are being so ridiculously cautious, that millions will suffer if they get their way. They do not care what science says, especially when it tells them that they are wrong.

The precautionary principle also causes harm by encouraging massive spending to correct problems of limited or negligible impact, leaving less funding for other measures that could be more important. Cleanups are accomplished only by diverting resources from other worthy missions, including the avoidance of other health risks.[9] For example, putting the $6 billion per year being spent on Superfund cleanups toward cancer research would quadruple cancer research spending.[10] Estimates have put the cost of cancer prevented through Superfund cleanup at greater than $10 billion per case.[11] In other words, to prevent one case of cancer, the Superfund has spent $10 billion. How many actual lives could have been saved if these funds were put into cancer research?

Another example: vast amounts of resources have been devoted to cleaning up lead at hazardous waste sites, while more significant exposures such as apartment paint and soil in urban areas have received much less attention.[12]

The precautionary principle as a guide to decision making suffers from another drawback. As noted by Wilfred Beckerman: "If the future is really all that uncertain, how can one be confident that action today will not make things worse, rather than better?" [12]

If reform and regulations are to be based on the precautionary principle, the following must be kept in mind.

1. Not every risk is avoidable.

2. All risks are relative.

3. Wealthier is healthier. Actions which lower living standards typically increase risk and shorten life expectancy.

4. Regulations can have adverse side effects, thus creating more risk and less protection.

5. More lives would be saved if risks were prioritized.[9]

Application of the precautionary principle makes sense if it is done with these five principles in mind, but policymakers who use the strongest definitions of the precautionary principle turn a blind eye to the risk by overregulation. Jonathan Adler believes this is a costly mistake. "For much of the world, the greatest environmental threats derive from poverty and a lack of innovation, not newfangled technologies. By focusing only on those risks posed by the uncertainties of new technologies, the precautionary principle turns a blind eye to the harms that occur, or are made worse, by the lack of technological development."[13]

References

1. Terry F. Yosie, "Science-Based Decision Making at The Crossroads," *Vital Speeches*, LXVII (January 15,2001), 216

2. Kenneth R. Foster, Paolo Vecchia and Michael H. Repacholi, "Science and the Precautionary Principle," *Science*, 288 (May 12, 2000), 979

3.   Aaron Wildavsky, "Trial and Error Versus Trial Without Error," in *Rethinking Risk and the Precautionary Principle*, ed. Julian Morris (Oxford, Butterworth Heinemann, 2000), 27

4.   Henry I. Miller and Gregory Conko, "Genetically Modified Fear and the International Regulation of Biotechnology," in *Rethinking Risk and the Precautionary Principle*, ed. Julian Morris (Oxford, Butterworth Heinemann, 2000), 100

5.   John Brignell, *Sorry, Wrong Number,* (Great Britain, Brignell Associates, 2000), 194

6.   Melinda Muse, *I'm Afraid, You're Afraid; 448 Things to Fear and Why*, (New York, Hyperion, 2000), 152

7.   Aaron Wildavsky, "Trial and Error Versus Trial Without Error," in *Rethinking Risk and the Precautionary Principle*, ed. Julian Morris (Oxford, Butterworth Heinemann, 2000), 42

8.   James M. Taylor, "Anti-chlorine activists hope politics will trump science," *Environment and Climate News*, 5, (October 2002), 1

9.   John C. Shanahan and Adam D. Thierer, "How to Talk About Risk: How Well Intentioned Regulations Can Kill," *The Heritage Foundation*, Report No. 13 (April 23, 1996)

10.   *Cutting Green Tape*, eds. Richard L. Stroup and Roger E. Meiners, (Oakland, California, The Independent Institute, 2000), 10

11.   *Cutting Green Tape*, eds. Richard L. Stroup and Roger E. Meiners, (Oakland, California, The Independent Institute, 2000), xv

12.   Wilfred Beckerman, "The Precautionary Principle and Our Obligations to Future Generations," in *Rethinking Risk and the Precautionary Principle*, ed. Julian Morris (Oxford, Butterworth Heinemann, 2000), 53

13.   Johnathan H. Adler, "Better Safe Than Sorry?", *Intellecual Ammunition*, (Chicago, The Heartland Institute, November/December 1999), 6

Chapter 17

The Cost of a Life and Interventions

How much is a single human life worth? Are the returns (i.e. number of lives saved) of risk reduction worth the cost? Is the life of an animal worth more than that of a human being?

At the very least, these are all loathsome questions. Let's look at the amounts of money spent on environmental programs and tally what a life is worth, human and animal alike.

Assigning a dollar value to life may seem repugnant, but we all do it frequently. When we decide not to have occasional medical checkups, when we buy low priced tires instead of the ones that do not blow out, when we drive compact cars rather than large ones that can better withstand a crash we place a dollar value on saving our own lives and those of others.[1]

First, here is a sampling of what very small sums of money can do to save lives. According to the World Health Organization (WHO), for as little as $1 per patient per year, the world could eliminate four tropical diseases by 2007 – leprosy, Chagas' disease, river blindness and lymphatic filarisis.[2] WHO also states that a life can be saved for $20 in Indonesia or $50 in Gambia. In various Third World countries it is possible by spending $550 to save a life from malaria, $2,000 on general health care, $4,000 on water sanitation or $5,000 on improved nutrition.[3]

Approximately 5 million people die each year from diarrhea in underdeveloped countries. It is estimated that 50 to 75% of these deaths could be prevented by oral therapy (ORT).[1] This involves drinking a mixture of glucose, salt, baking soda, and water. These salts restore the body's electrolyte balance and the degree of salinity in the cells, allowing the cells to retain fluid. Christopher J. Drasbek of the Pan American Health Organization reports that for $500,000, 2.5 million lives could be saved annually. As P.J. O'Rourke points out: "This is about half the cost of a 30 second Superbowl commercial - an apt comparison since Gatorade is more or less a commercial version of oral rehydration therapy (although the precise clinical effect of dumping it on coaches is not fully understood.)"[4]

These are inexpensive ways to save lives. Imagine, for the cost of 15 seconds of air time at the Superbowl, 2.5 million lives could be saved in underdeveloped countries by drinking Gatorade. It boggles the mind.

Now let's take a look at the cost effectiveness of different strategies here in the United States for saving lives. The best way to start is through a table comparing life saving costs for third world countries, with some environnmental and non-environmental life saving activities in the U.S. As you will see, the inefficiency of environmental regulations is clearly evident. In other words, as Gabor Levy says: "These exhorbitant sums are not spent, but rather it would take centuries by statistical extrapolation and huge investements before a single life would be saved."[5]

The key findings of these tables are that the return on investment for different kinds of "risk reduction" opportunities varies enormously. Clearly, environmental interventions are the most costly and least efficient. It is still repugnant to assign a dollar value to each life saved, but does this make for sound economic policy? Shouldn't more money be spent in areas that are more efficient, and save more lives? For instance, there are several measures that cost less than $1 per life-year saved. Among these are: an improved standard for concrete construction; flammability standards for children's sleepware; measles, mumps, and rubella vaccinations; and reduction of lead in gasoline from 1.1 to 0.1 g/gal.[6]

As seen in Table 17.1, the most expensive environmental regulations (interventions) can be labeled as "toxic control." Unfortunately, this approach to toxic control ends up killing more people than it protects. As Justice Stephen Breyer observed, there is an income effect from spending money on nonproductive activities like cleaning dirt. "At all times regulation imposes costs that mean less real income available to individuals for alternative expenditure. That deprivation of real income itself has adverse health effects, in the form of poorer diet, more heart attacks, more suicides."[7] Philip Howard discloses: "Every 1% increase in unemployment over time is correlated with 19,000 more deaths by heart attack, and 1,100 more suicides. That works out to about 4 unnecessary deaths for the $30 million spent on a typical cleanup, and 14 deaths on a $100 million regulation that saves 1 life."[8]

Table 17.1: Costs to Save a Life

Activity	Costs Per Death Averted
THIRD WORLD COUNTRIES[a]	
Diptheria Immunization (Gambia)	$87
Measles Immunization (Ivory Coast)	$850
Improved Health Care	$1,930
Improved Water Sanitation	$4,030
Dietary Supplements	$5,300
UNITED STATES, NON-ENVIRONMENTAL[a]	
Improved Traffic Signs	$31 thousand
Cervical Cancer Screening	$50 thousand
Improved Lighting	$80 thousand
Upgrade Guard Rails	$101 thousand
Mobile Intensive Care Units	$120 thousand
Breakaway Sign Supports	$125 thousand
Lung Cancer Screening	$140 thousand
Breast Cancer Screening	$160 thousand
UNITED STATES, ENVIRONMENTAL[b]	
Acrylonitrile emission control via best technology	$9 million
Arsenic emission control (glass manufacturing)	$51 million
Ban asbestos in acetylene cylinders	$350 million
Benzene emission control (tire manufacturing)	$20 billion
Radionuclide emission control (uranium fuel cycle plants)	$34 billion
Chloroform private well emission standard (49 pulp mills)	$99 billion

(a) Bernard L. Cohen, "Perspectives on the Cost Effectiveness of Life Saving," in *Rational Readings on Environmental Concerns*, ed., Jay H. Lehr (New York, Van Nostrand Reinhold, 1992), 461
(b) Tammy O. Tengs, et. al., "Five Hundred Life Saving Interventions and Their Cost-Effectiveness," Risk Analysis, 15 (1995), 369

Table 17.2: Median of Cost Per Life Year Saved Estimates as a Function of Sector of Society and Type of Intervention[a]

Sector of Society	Intervention Costs
Health Care	$19 thousand
Residential	$36 thousand
Transportation	$56 thousand
Occupational	$350 thousand
Environmental	$2.8 million

(a) Tammy O. Tengs, et. al., "Five Hundred Life Saving Interventions and Their Cost-Effectiveness," Risk Analysis, 15 (1995), 369

Table 17.3: Median Cost-Effectiveness of Proposed Government Regulations[a]

Agency	Median Cost/Life-Year
Federal Aviation Administration	$23 thousand
Consumer Product Safety Commission	$68 thousand
National Highway Traffic Safety Administration	$78 thousand
Occupational Health and Safety Administration	$88 thousand
Environmental Protection Agency	$7.6 million

(a) Tammy O. Tengs, et. al., "Five Hundred Life Saving Interventions and Their Cost-Effectiveness," Risk Analysis, 15 (1995), 369

The study by Tammy Tengs and her co-authors conducted at the Harvard Center for Risk Analysis (see Tables 2-3 and Environmental section of Table I) was used to create a database, based on figures mostly from scientific journals and goverment regulatory impact analyses. After the initial study resulting in the numbers and facts we have discussed to this point, a follow-on paper addressed the issue of how many lives could be saved annually if we invested the same amount of money on interventions shown to save the greatest number of lives possible. They found that 60,000 lives are lost every year in the United States due to "wasteful allocation of resources."[9]

Lastly, I want to broach the final question of the opening to this chapter. Is the life of an animal worth more than that of a human being? Before we start to look at the numbers, I want to share a quick story that might answer the question right from the start.

Mike Davis reports the following in *Ecology of Fear*: "Mountain Lions, whom wildlife experts call 'the Rolls Royce of North American Predators,' have their share of defenders. After 40 year old Barbara Schoener was killed and partially devoured by a female mountain lion while hiking in a Sierra recreation area, 45 miles north of Sacramento, there was an extraordinary outpouring of empathy for the animal (subsequently killed by trackers). Sympathizers reportedly donated twice as much to a fund for the lion's orphaned cubs than to the fund for Schoener's two small children.[10]

On to the numbers. Below in Table 17.4, you will see the costs (so far) of protecting endangered and threatened species in the U.S.

There is no debate that animals are important, but are these expenses better spent elsewhere? Following are several examples of programs, large and small scale, that seem to have been utter wastes of resources.

Table 17.4: Dollars Spent to Preserve and Recover Endangered and Threatened Species[a]

Species	Cost
California Condor	$40 million[b]
Northern Spotted Owl	$9.7 million
Least Bell's Vireo (bird)	$9.2 million
Grizzly Bear	$5.9 million
Red Cockaded Woodpecker	$5.2 million
Florida Panther	$4.1 million
Mojave Desert Tortoise	$4.1 million
Bald Eagle	$3.5 million
Ocelot	$3.0 million
Jaguarundi (wild cat)	$2.9 million
American Peregrine Falcon	$2.9 million

(a) Dixy Lee Ray and Lou Guzzo, *Environmental Overkill*, (New York, Harper Perennial, 1993), 90
(b) Jane Kay, "California Condor's Comeback," San Francisco Chronicle, (January 14, 2002), F1

In many places, people build pathways or tunnels to try to prevent animals from contacting automobiles. Peter Kafka describes some of these activities: worried that we are losing too many frogs, toads and other amphibians under the wheels of cars, environmentalists from Texas to Germany have hit upon a dubious solution – building express tunnels that let the crossing critters crawl underneath the highway." Kafka also discusses a $40,000 project aimed at finding out how to design a tunnel that will bisect a stretch of U.S. Highway 319 outisde Tallahassee, Florida. The major problem with this approach...figuring out how to guide the gopher frog and striped newt through the portal. Also, the underpass must be wide enough and tall enough, with a grate so the animals can see the sky.[13] As of March 2002 the underpass had not been built, but the number of species and amphibians and reptiles that would be affected now numbered 27.[14]

"The City of Davis, California spent $12,000 on a toad tunnel in 1996, but no one seems to know if it has worked. 'I don't really know and I don't know if anybody's gone over there to check,' admits Davis Mayor Pro Tem Julie Portansky who first advocated the tunnel when she was on the city concil."[13]

Florida has built passageways under roads in the Everglades for al-ligators (alligator alleys?). It also has built miles of fences in the Everglades to keep the Florida panther from darting in front of automobiles. Do these precautions work? In Florida I have seen many alligators hanging around these passageways and have never seen an alligator road kill. But, Lorna Rewis, who has spent 60 years in the area where the fences were built, has never seen a panther in the region.[15]

Between 1969 and 1973, the New Mexico Game and Fish Department released 93 African oryx (a large antelope) in the White Sands Missile Range as part of its exotic animal introduction program. Researchers predicted that the population would never grow beyond 500 to 600 and would remain within the Tularosa basin. However, the animals reached a population of 5,000 or more, and have been spotted from 60 miles south of Albuquerque all the way down to West Texas. Since they breed year round and don't have African lions to prey on them, they are thriving.[16]

In 1996 because of overgrazing and other problems with the oryx, the Park Service spent $1,040,000 on 67.6 miles of fencing to completely close the 225 miles of the White Sands National Monument to keep the animals out.[16] However, Murphy's Law was in effect and over 200 animals were inadvertently fenced in. The Park Service then let it be known that it was considering shooting the remaining animals. This alerted animal rights activists and forced the agency to resort to live trapping at a cost of $400,000. Despite the success of this effort, some 12 to 20 animals still remain in the park. As of July 13, 2002 plans were to shoot the remaining oryx.[17]

Calipatria, a "level four" maximum security state prison in California currently houses some 4,000 inmates. However, there is a noticeable absence of surveillance. Ten of the facility's 12 perimeter gun towers are unmanned as is the guard booth at the main gate. But, don't worry about convicts escaping. The facility is surrounded by a 13 foot electric fence, sandwiched between two ordinary chain link fences. Each of the individual strands that are part of the electric fence bristle with 5,000 volts, about 10 times the recognized lethal dosage. When the fence was activated in 1993, prison folks were pleased. However, they had neglected to factor the animal-rights people into the equation. As Davis explains, "The prison is just east of the Salton Sea, a major wintering habitat for waterfowl, and the gently purring high voltage fence immediately became an erotic beacon to passing birds. Local bird watchers soon found out about the body count (all of five birds: one gull, two owls, one finch, and a scissor-tailed flycatcher) and alerted the Audubon society. By January, Calipatria's 'death fence' was an international environmental scandal. When a CNN crew pulled into the prison parking lot, the Department of Corrections threw in the towel and hired an ornithologist to help them redesign the fence." Davis further points out that the result is the world's only birdproof, ecologically responsible death fence. The innovations include a warning wire for curious rodents, anti-perching deflectors for wildfowl, and tiny passageways for burrowing owls, all at a cost of $150,000.[18]

Oil spills also lead to massively expensive efforts to rescue animals. When they occur we often see and hear about oil-soaked birds. Here's what Marguerite Holloway says about cleaning up these creatures, "Ultimately, it is the frame of the television set and the mind-set of the media about oiled animals. The public wants the animals saved — at about $80,000 per otter and $10,000 per bird — even if the stress of their salvation kills them.[19]

High on the present list of most expensive animals has to be the Canadian lynx, which is currently receiving much attention. As reported by Rex Dalton in Nature, "A study of the habitat of the threatened Canadian lynx in U.S. forests is embroiled in fierce controversy, after it emerged that wildlife biologists sent fur samples from captive lynx to a laboratory that was supposed to be monitoring the whereabouts of the animals in the wild.[20] Five U.S. Federal and two Washington State Fish and Wildlife researchers were caught planting hair samples from a threatened Canadian lynx in an American national forest. The researchers were conducting a four year study of 57 forests in 16 states to determine the extent of lynx habitat. This has led to "political rhetoric flying like fur at a feline fracas."[21]

Most reports are strongly critical of the biologists.[20, 22-24] With statements such as, "The public has a right to know who attempted this huge economic sabotage," Center for the Defense of Free Enterprise Executive Vice President Ron Arnold added, "We need to know their names so we can trace any direct links to agenda driven environment groups in Washington state and elsewhere that have worked for years to shut down resource industries and motorized recreation, and they know the Canadian lynx is the perfect surrogate for their political goals. Rural areas across America could have been stripped of virtually all economic and recreational use, costing millions of dollars in lost jobs, goods, and services."[22]

Although a report in Nature says the "lynching is undeserved," we will undoubtedly hear more about this issue.[21] This isn't the first time lynx have made national headlines. Dan Whipple reported in *Audubon* in 1999, "The future of lynx and the Vail resort in Colorado was intertwined in a tangled tale of skiiing, politics, and the costliest act of ecoterrorism in history. On October 19, 1998, members of the Earth Liberation Front (ELF) set fires on two ridgetops at Vail, causing an estimated $12 million in damage to two restaurants and four ski lifts. The fires blazed just two days after Vail Associates, owner of the ski resort, began clearing trees for a 900 acre expansion in the area where lynx were last seen. An e-mail from the ELF said the fires were set on behalf of the lynx."[25] One can only wonder if there is a connection among all these activites on behalf of the lynx. In a related item, the Wall Street Journal reported the following; "Hot on the heels of environmental scandals over lynx data, sucker fish and salmon habitats, comes news that Forest Service officials knowingly used false data about spotted owls to block logging in a California forest. Federal Judge Lawrence S. Margolis ruled the agency's action was 'arbitrary, capricious and without rational basis,' and that the officials knew their data was faulty even as they ordered the sales cancelled. The federal government recently agreed to pay the logging company, Wetsel-Oviatt, $9.5 million for four cancelled sales."[26]

All too often we spend more money to save animals than to help people in need. No debate that animals are important, but are they really more important than human lives? Or is the life not as important if we don't see it, e.g. in a poor section of one of our cities or in a Third World Country.

Mark Dowie quotes Dorceta Taylor, a professor of sociology in the School of Natural Resources at the University of Michigan; "If it is discovered that birds have lost their nesting sites, environmentalists go to great extremes to erect nesting boxes and find alternate breeding sites for them. When whales are stranded, enormous sums are spent to provide them food. When forests are threatened, large numbers of people are mobilized to prevent damage. But we have yet to see an environmental group champion human homelessness or joblessness as issues on which they will spend vast resources. It is a strange paradox that a movement that exhorts the harmonious coexistence of people and nature, worries about the continued survival of nature (particularly loss of habitat problems) somehow forgets about the survival of humans, especially those who have lost their habitats or food sources. If this trend continues a vital piece of the web of survival will be missing."[27]

Certainly this has been a difficult chapter as we have tried to answer the questions posed in the beginning. There is mounting evidence that environmental regulations and interventions cost a lot of money, with little positive effect (i.e. # of lives saved) as opposed to programs that have definitive positive effects and cost much less. We have also seen that in many cases, environmental groups have overreacted or outright lied in order to keep their agenda rolling. What is the answer?

References

1. Bernard L. Cohen, "Perspectives on the Cost Effectiveness of Life Saving," in *Rational Readings on Environmental Concerns*, ed., Jay H. Lehr, (New York, Van Nostrand Reinhold, 1992), 461

2. Lauren Neergaard, "Four tropical diseases can be cheaply eradicated, WHO says," *Los Angeles Times*, (Sunday March 16, 1997), D1

3. Jay H. Lehr, "A New Measure of Risk," in *Rational Readings on Environmental Concerns*, ed., Jay H. Lehr, (New York, Van Nostrand Reinhold, 1992), 689

4. P.J. O'Rourke, *All the Trouble in the World*, (New York, Atlantic Monthly Press, 1994), 269

5. Gabor B. Levy, "A Very Sick Horse," *American Laboratory*, (January 1995), 8

6. Tammy O. Tengs, et. al., "Five Hundred Life Saving Interventions and Their Cost-Effectiveness," *Risk Analysis*, 15, (1995), 369

7. Stephen Breyer, *Breaking the Vicious Circle*, (Cambridge, Massachusetts, Harvard University Press, 1993), 23

8. Philip K. Howard, *The Death of Common Sense*, (New York, Random House, 1994), 47

9. Tammy O. Tengs and John D. Graham, "The Opportunity of Haphazard Social Investments in Life-Saving," in *Risks, Costs, and Lives Saved*, ed., Robert W. Hahn, (Oxford, England, Oxford University Press, 1996), 167

10. Mike Davis, *Ecology of Fear,* (New York, Metropolitan Books, 1998), 201

11. Dixy Lee Ray and Lou Guzzo, *Environmental Overkill*, (New York, Harper Perennial, 1993), 90

12. Jane Kay, "California Condor's Comeback," *San Francisco Chronicle*, (January 14, 2002), F1

13. Peter Kafka, "Environmental Tunnel Vision," *Forbes*, 161, (May 4, 1998), 39

14. D. Bruce Means, Coastal Plains Institute and Land Conservancy, private communication with author, March 22, 2002

15. Lorna Rewis, "Local History and Folklore of the 10,000 Islands Wilderness in Everglades National Park," talk given to the Elderhostel Program, December 7, 2000

16. Robert Rowley, "A Graceful Gazelle Becomes A Pest," *High Country News*, Volume 33, (October 22, 2001)

17. "Finding of No Significant Impact; Complete the Removal of African Oryx, White Sands National Monument, New Mexico," http://data.itc.nps.gov/parks/whsa/ppdocuments/oryx_FONSI.htm, accessed July 13, 2002

18. Mike Davis, *Ecology of Fear*, 412

19. Marguerite Holloway, "Sounding Out Science," *Scientific American*, 275, (October 1996), 106

20. Rex Dalton, "Fur flies over lynx survey's suspect samples," *Nature*, 415, (January 10, 2002), 107

21. "Lynch mob turns on lynx researchers," *Nature*, 415, (January 10, 2002), 101

22. Leesa Kiewl, "The great lynx hair hoax — Federal employees plant bogus evidence and conspire to commit fraud!", *Agri-News*, Billings, Montana, (January 11, 2002), 1

23. James M. Taylor, "Gov't researchers caught planting false ESA evidence," *Environment & Climate News*, 5, (March 2002), 1

24. Audrey Hudson, "GAO: Lynx fur hoax was no secret," *The Washington Times*, March 7, 2002

25. Dan Whipple, "Hot Lynx in Vail," *Audubon*, 101, (January-February 1999), 14

26. "Unspotted Owls," *The Wall Street Journal*," (March 21, 2002), A22

27. Mark Dowie, *Losing Ground*, (Cambridge, Massachusetts, The MIT Press, 1997), 126

Chapter 18

One in a Million — Human Health Risk

A message for all women in the workplace. You are breaking the law.

Of course, I am kidding, but it brings up a point. If we apply the **one in a million** criterion currently employed by several government agencies to women in the workplace, they would have to be banned from having jobs because the chance of a woman being killed at work is 1 in 600,000.

One in a million (10^{-6}) is used to assess human health risks. According to Kathryn Kelly and Nanette Cardon, the past, present and future costs of complying with the stringent standard are virtually incalculable. "It is difficult to imagine a criterion in wider use in the U.S." Some examples where it is used include:[1]

- pesticides in food additives
- allowable exposure to groundwater contamination and incinerators
- emissions from stacks
- how a hazardous waste site should be cleaned up
- how much Alar to leave on apples

Kelly and Cardon further state: "Lifetime exposure to a substance associated with a risk of 10^{-6} would increase our current chances of developing cancer which is about one in three, by 0.0003 percent."[1] Stated another way, the regulatory agencies are attempting to reduce the cancer incidence of 300,000 people to 299,999.[2] Problems arise with assigning a specific figure to the number of cases of cancer considered acceptable. As Alice Ottoboni points out: "It gives the public a false impression that the figure is a matter of scientific fact rather than a statistically derived estimate. It delivers the erroneous message that one in a million people, no more, no less, will actually develop cancer from exposure to the chemical in question. It misleads the public into believing that one extra case of cancer in a population of a million people actually could be measured and the cause could be identified. Finally, it frightens some people who fear that they or one of their loved ones may become that one unfortunate soul in a million."[3]

Since many billions of dollars have been spent in attempting to achieve the one in a million (10^{-6}) goal for cleanups of hazardous waste sites in the United States, a good question would be, what is the scientific origin of 10^{-6}?

Answer. There is no sound scientific, social, economic, or other basis for the selection of 10^{-6} as a cleanup goal for hazardous waste sites. Extensive research by Kelly and Cardon led them to state: "Remarkably, the criterion, which has cost society billions of dollars, has never received widespread debate or even thorough regulatory or scientific review. It is an arbitrary level proposed 35 years ago for completely different regulations (animal drug residues), the circumstances of which do not apply to hazardous waste site regulation. As a result, implementing it has frequently been socially, politically, technically, and economically infeasible."[1]

The review conducted by Kelly and Cardon included an informal telephone survey of affected agencies and an extensive literature search. They found that: "None of the officials contacted at any Federal or state agency currently using 10^{-6} as a criterion knew the basis of this criterion, nor is there any readily available documentation that specifically described the origin of 10^{-6}." They discovered that "the concept of 10^{-6} was originally an arbitrary number finalized by the U.S. Food and Drug Administration as a screening level of 'essentially zero' or *deminimis* risk. This concept was traced back to a 1961 proposal by two scientists from the National Cancer Institute regarding methods to determine 'safety' levels in carcinogenicity testing."[1]

So how is 10^{-6} used? Interestingly, the risk level of 10^{-6} is not consistently applied to all environmental legislation. Instead, it seems to be applied according to the general perception of the risk associated with the source being regulated. Hazardous waste sites, pesticides, and selected carcinogens have seen almost exclusive application of 10^{-6}, while air, drinking water, or other sources perceived to be of less risk have not been subjected to this requirement.[1] Kelly and Cardon also report: "Cleanup levels for a contaminant are not consistent from site to site and vary by orders of magnitude." Furthermore, in some cases, there are extreme differences even among divisions of the same agency for the same substance. A case in point is arsenic, where there are six orders of magnitude (one million fold) difference in target risk within different EPA regulations.[1,4]

Let's take a look at other events or activities that increase our chance of death by one in a million.[5]

- smoking 1.4 cigarettes (cancer, heart disease)
- traveling 10 miles by bicycle (accident)
- traveling 300 miles by car (accident)
- traveling 1,000 miles by commercial aircraft (accident)
- playing with fireworks (accident)[6]
- drinking a half liter of wine (cirrhosis of the liver)
- traveling 6 minutes by canoe (accident)
- one chest X-ray (cancer)
- Eating 40 tablespoons of peanut butter (liver cancer from aflatoxin B)
- Eating 100 charbroiled steaks (cancer from benzyprene)

There is a one in a million chance that an asteroid with a diameter of 10^4 meters (Mt. Everest size) will hit the earth. If it did, the fatalities would range from 10 million to more than 1 billion people. So here's another one in a million item to consider. As Clark Chapman and David Morrison have stated, a typical U.S. citizen's risk of death from a killer rock from space is much higher that the widely publicized threats from certain carcinogens and poisoning by commercial foods.[6]

Carl Sagan said, "The odds of a miraculous cure at Lourdes are about one in a million. You are roughly as likely to recover after visiting Lourdes as you are to win the lottery, or to die in the crash of a regularly scheduled airplane flight — including the one taking you to Lourdes."[7]

There is no argument here against cleaning up hazardous waste sites or keeping pesticides out of the food stream. That would be foolish to even consider. Yet, how foolish is it that government agencies regulate using a standard (10^{-6}) that is both arbitrary and scientifically base-less? Even more so, how foolish is it to spend hundreds of billions of dollars to enforce these regulations, when your chances of becoming ill are the same as your chances of getting clocked over the head with chunks of rock from space?

References

1. Kathryn A. Kelly and Nanette C. Cardon, "The myth of 10^{-6} as a definition of aceptable risk," *EPA Watch*, Volume 3, Number 17, (September 15, 1994), 4

2. Bruce Yandle, "Human Health and Costly Risk Reduction," *The Freeman*, Volume 45, Number 3, (March 1995), 174

3. M. Alice Ottoboni, *The Dose Makes the Poison*, Second Edition, (New York, Van Nostrand Reinhold, 1997), 184

4. Curtis C. Travis, et al., "Cancer risk management," *Environmental Science & Technology*, 21, (1987), 415

5. Richard Wilson, "Analyzing the daily risks of life," *Technology Review*, 81, (February 1979), 41

6. Clark R. Chapman and David Morrison, "Impacts on the Earth by asteroids and comets: assessing the hazard," *Nature*, 367, (January 6, 1994), 33

7. Carl Sagan, *The Demon-Haunted World*, (New York, Random House, 1995), 233

Chapter 19

The EPA's Fat Chance

Tobacco smoke — 400,000 annual casualties, ranking first among "controllable killers" of humans in America. Alcohol — 100,000 annual casualties, ranking third. In second place? Well, certainly, if the environmentalists and media are right, it should be something like Alar, ozone depletion, dioxins, nuclear waste, electromagnetic radiation, pesticide residues, PCBs, or asbestos, shouldn't it?

Nope. Fat is the number two controllable killer of humans in America. "The problem is obesity, and it kills an estimated 300,000 Americans a year. A third of American adults are now classified as obese, defined as being at least 20 percent fatter than they should be. A quarter of our children are obese."[1]

Food is the culprit, and obesity is the symptom. Since food is such an enormous killer, it should be treated the same way we have treated other suspected killers such as Alar, asbestos, pesticides, etc. We need a bunch of laws that allow the Environmental Protection Agency (EPA) to control and monitor our food consumption to reduce the number of deaths annually. Not only would we save thousands of lives, but could probably do so for much less than the EPA spends to save one.

We've talked about the costs of the EPA and other government agencies to save lives in previous chapters. To quickly reiterate with an example, the rules and regulations governing the exposure to formaldehyde set up by OSHA amounts to a cost of $86 billion to avert a single case of cancer.[2] I'm hoping that saving obese people won't cost that much. Hopefully it will be closer to the following examples.

Michael Gough and Steven Milloy make the following observations. "Tammy O. Tengs and her colleagues at the Harvard Center for Risk Analysis examined the costs of 500 'life saving interventions,' which were defined as 'any behavioral and/or premature death among a specified target population.' They calculated that the median cost of an intervention for each life-year saved was $42,000, with an enormous range: the median cost of a medical intervention to save a life-year was $19,000; and the median cost of injury reduction was $48,000.[3] Those numbers are bit better.

So, here are my proposals to the EPA on how to save obese Americans.

1. Set up a structure of fines and prison sentences such as have been used in the past and present for regulation violators. Certainly, the thought of prison time will be an excellent deterrent and obese people would be more inclined to watch their diets.

2. EPA statisticians could provide tables outlining what a desirable weight is, and how much weight would have to be lost in a given amount of time for those with excess pounds.

3. Use a Goodwill program. For example, the EPA's 33/50 program in which industries voluntarily reduced toxics by 33 percent in two years and by 50 percent in four years could serve as a model. The language could simply be changed to a 33 percent reduction in excess pounds in two years and a 50 percent reduction in four years. Perhaps reductions of lesser magnitude could be used to make the goal realistically attainable.

4. Use the Common Sense Initiative. The original Common Sense Initiative was designed to bring together the EPA, selected industrial representatives, environmental and public interest research groups, and state/local regulators in a cooperative effort to increase efficiency, while reducing the economic burden the EPA's programs were placing on industry. The initiative sought to develop a more responsive system of environmental protection that was "cleaner, cheaper and smarter." Clearly, a Common Sense Initiative for the overweight could be implemented and would be very successful, since it would show good will on behalf of both the EPA and volunteers.

With a third of Americans classified as obese, the challenge for the EPA would be mind boggling. Clearly, if it took advantage of this opportunity, it could improve its statistics (lives saved per dollar spent) immeasurably. Here are some of the problems I see, and hope the EPA will have the foresight to meet the challenges head on.

1. Bureaucracy. If we think the current EPA staff (~18,000) is big now, think of how enormous it will have to be to police one out of every three individuals.

2. Personnel. Officers of the EPA will have to be what is considered "svelte," as an obese officer should not be enforcing rules on obesity. Obviously, there will be discrimination lawsuits because of selective hiring, and body style profiling.

3. Lawsuits. Besides the hiring problems, there would certainly be many difficulties with overweight acceptance groups protesting the work of the EPA officers.

4. Unemployment. What about all the people who profit from diet fads? Sales figures for diet books, videos, and audio cassettes were over $1 billion by the end of 2000. This doesn't include all the special products supposedly designed to reduce weight.[4] What will happen to all these people that make and sell these products? Perhaps this is the perfect employment pool and will solve #2.

The trials and tribulations of the EPA in trying to wipe out the nation's number two controllable killer will be many, but I think they have a chance.

Of course, I am kidding, but I hope you see how ridiculous it is that the EPA continues to spend billions and billions of dollars to save one life, or avert one case of sickness. It is uncontrolled spending and it needs to stop.

Oh, one last thing, a bit of advice for the EPA. That "end-of-pipe" strategy that you use...checking the waste at the source of its exit...isn't advisable here.

References

1. Michael Fumento, *The Fat of the Land*, (New York, Viking, 1997), xv

2. Dixy Lee Ray, "Environmental Regulation: Costs & Benefits," (Washington, D.C., George C. Marshall Institute, March 1993), 5

3. Michael Gough and Steven Milloy, "EPA's Cancer Risk Guidelines: Guidance to Nowhere," *Policy Analysis*, No. 263, (Washington, D.C., Cato Institute, November 12, 1996), 10

4. Michael Fumento, *The Fat of the Land*, 131

Section 5:

Radiation and Cancer Risk

Chapter 20

Radiation — It's What You Think You Know

Radiation. The word itself can bring shivers to even the most hardy individuals, but it shouldn't. As Mark Twain said, "It isn't what we don't know that causes the problems, it's what we think we know that just isn't so." The fear of radiation comes from the many doomsayers that have used an unwitting press and public to their advantage for decades.

Have you ever heard?

- Low levels of radiation are beneficial to humans.
- Mice exposed to low levels of radiation lived longer than mice that were not.
- Fish exposed to low levels of radiation grew faster than fish that weren't.
- Low levels of radiation increase fertility and embryo viability, and decrease sterility and mutations. [1]

It's more likely that you have heard the following. When radioactivity from the Chernobyl accident reached our West Coast, the press warned residents about the dangers of possible fallout; speaking of the number of picocuries of radioactivity detected in high clouds without ever explaining that a picocurie is one part per trillion. To use a dollars-and-cents analogy, a curie can be measured as one-fifth of the U.S. federal budget ($5 trillion). A picocurie is the cost of a hamburger and Coke. According to Dixy Lee Ray, fomer head of the Atomic Energy Commission, the press also never mentioned that you would have to drink 63,000 gallons of that radioactive rain water to ingest one picocurie of radioactivity. [2]

Perhaps you heard about the "nuclear disaster" at Three Mile Island (TMI). The press covered this nonstop, and it is still used by antinuclear groups as the biggest reason to trash all nuclear power plants. A report by the Nuclear Regulatory Commission (NRC) revealed that the average dose of radiation received by two million people in the surrounding area was 0.0014 rems. The highest estimated individual exposure resulting from the TMI release was 0.075 rems. Here's the rub. A typical person in the United States receives about 0.36 rems of radiation annually from naturally occurring radiation, medical uses of radiation, and consumer products.[3] You get five times more radiation every year just by being alive! As Edward Remmers points out: "The most serious damage from Three Mile Island was the psychological trauma and over-exaggeration from the mishandling of this incident by politicians and the media."[4]

Okay, so what's a rem? A rem is the amount of energy deposited in the human body by ionizing radiation. For ease of understanding, Mark Hart of the Lawrence Livermore National Laboratory equates 1 rem to 1 dollar, so 1 millirem is 0.1 cents or 1/10th of a cent. The yearly limit for safe exposure is 5 rem, or 5 dollars.[5] Hart has worked in a plutonium facility over a period of six years, and he frequently presents a talk entitled "Radiation-What Is Important?" In this talk, which he often gives to children, he uses over 100 radioactive items, including antiques, consumer items, fossils, and minerals. After his talk it is hard for me to imagine anyone, except the hardest core environmentalist, who has not changed some of his or her thinking about radiation.

Hart has yet to go into an antique store where he did not find something that was radioactive. However, he points out that there is no danger from radiation in antiques, even when used as food plates. Cindy Cassady reports this from an interview with Hart. "One of the most important aspects of radiation is the public's perception," said Hart as he drank coffee from an antique radioactive coffee cup made of green 'Depression' glass. The key factor, he discloses, is that the radioactive material stays in the glass and does not enter his body. "These radioactive items won't make other things radioactive." His collection of plates, cups, glasses, cases, jewelry, gravy boats, and baby dishes made of green or yellow glass popular in the 1920s and 30s or coated with orange uranium oxide glaze, all exhibit some degree of radiation above background and pose no health threat.[6]

Radioactivity is a perfectly natural phenomenon. The ground we walk on is radioactive; so is our blood; so is the food we eat; so is the air we breathe.[7] At what elevation do you live? For every 100 meter increase in altitude, the annual radiation dose increases by approximately 1.5 millirem. This increase occurs because, as elevation increases, there is less atmosphere to shield the secondary cosmic radiation.[8] Therefore, Denver's exposure is approximately twice that of Washington, D.C. People residing in Rocky Mountain states receive twice the natural background radiation as people in other parts of the country, due to higher altitudes and large deposits of uranium. However, compared with states with lower natural background radiation, Rocky Mountain residents experience fewer age-adjusted overall cancer deaths and a lung cancer rate only two-thirds as high.[9]

Do you travel? Joe Bast and colleagues report: "A single coast to coast airplane flight subjects its passengers to 5 millirems of radiation in a single day, an amount equal to a full year's exposure by living next door to a nuclear reactor."[10] Yet the postulated danger of receiving an extra 10 millirems per year from living at the border of a radioactive waste site has received vastly more attention from the press and the public. Radiation exposure varies around the world. In Grand Central Station in New York it is 0.53 rems per year, while St. Peter's Square in Rome it is 0.80 rems per year. Note that the rules that will be applied in the decommissioning of U.S. nuclear power plants would require the stone structures of St. Peter's Square in Rome and Grand Central Station in New York to be dismantled and buried because of their radioactivity.[5]

In Ramsar, Iran the radiation level is 48 rem per year.[5] In 1990, this city was host to an international conference on high levels of natural radiation (HLNR). It makes sense to hold such a conference in a city with one of the highest natural radiation levels in the world. The conference was a continuation of a series of conferences held previously on this topic. One conclusion from this meeting was that epidemiological studies on HLNR in a number of countries did not show any evidence that people there were less healthy than in normal areas.[11]

Hot springs and mineral water resorts usually have elevated amounts of radioactivity. For example, the waters of the English city of Bath have a radon content of 1,730 picocuries(pCi) per liter. Compare this with the value of 4 pCi per liter that the EPA has set for homes. The radon in natural gas at Bath is 33,650 pCi per liter. Other places like Bath include Baden Baden, Warm Springs, Georgia and White Springs, Virginia.[12]

A report on residual radioactivity in the soil in Kazakhstan, at the site of the first Soviet nuclear explosion in August 1949, provides some interesting data. Altogether, 459 nuclear explosions were conducted at the three technical areas of this site between 1949 and 1989. Of these, 346 were underground explosions. All 113 of the other explosions, 26 ground and 87 atmospheric, occurred at a single area, Technical Area III.[13] In reviewing this work, Arthur Robinson reports: "Surely here we can find the nuclear hell on earth of unsurvivable residual radiation. Yet measurements revealed that one hour spent at the site of 113 nuclear explosions over a 40 year period ending in 1989 has about the same negative health effects from radiation as a trip from San Francisco to New York in an ordinary jetliner."[14]

So why are we so afraid of radiation? John Cameron says, "It is my belief that much of the blame for the public's fears and apprehensions with respect to radiation matters are due to our media. There is another criticism that must be directed to the media, namely, their constant use of a small number of individuals, who are clearly out of step with the radiation protection community. In the U.S. alone there are some 3,500 health physicists and 1,900 radiological physicists. Yet the media will, for some freshly breaking news story, seek out some half a dozen individuals who are willing to make willfully deceptive statements regarding radiation."

Cameron further says that out of a collection of "popular" books published over the last decade or so dealing with radiation matters there is not a single one that is not riddled with half-truths, outright lies, and evident ignorance of nuclear energy or radiation; another insidious practice designed to keep the public alarmed about radiation matters.[15]

It is true that very large amounts of radiation can cause cancer or even death. For that matter a large amount of anything, even water, is dangerous. However, all studies of low level radiation doses to humans indicate no harm, and many studies suggest that low level radiation is beneficial. *Radiation Hormesis* by T.D. Luckey is a 336 page compendium of actual observations showing beneficial effects of radiation in many aspects, with more than 1,000 references. We'll discuss radiation hormesis in the next chapter.

The two most widespread applications of nuclear energy, are electricity generation and the use of radioisotopes produced in nuclear reactors to diagnose many human conditions including cancer, cardiovascular disease, metabolic disorders and mental illness.[16] The use of nuclear energy to generate electricity has encountered so much opposition that no application for a nuclear power plant has been filed since the early 1970s. Yet, few people object to nuclear medicine or radiology even though their contribution to background radiation in the U.S. is a thousand times greater than discharges from the nuclear power industry.[17] There has not been a single fatal accident involving radiation in the U.S. for over 20 years, whereas there have been over 2 million fatalities from other types of accidents during the same period.[18] The loss of life expectancy from being 20 percent overweight is 900 days; while the loss of life expectancy from radiation emitted by nuclear power plants is 29 minutes.[19]

Many of the benefits that radiation offers, for example in health, safety and economic development, are frustrated by opposition from pressure groups encouraged by the media. In the United States, surveys continually place nuclear power at the top of the lists of risks in life.[20] The fact that nuclear power plants are seen as "accidents waiting to happen" has stifled this technology for over 20 years which is inexcusable. Just this last summer, news about brownouts and power outages in the hottest places in America were all over the airwaves. We have the ability to ensure these things never happen, and to bring safe, economical energy to everyone in this nation sitting right in front of us. But, activists use half-truths and outright lies to ensure we never use it.

Irrational fears have also blocked food irradiation. We would not be reading about the latest E. coli contamination in food if irradiation were used. To combat this public health problem, the US Department of Agriculture began to allow the use of irradiation to treat meats.[21] However, activists have prevented this from taking hold to a great extent.

Using politics to trump science, activists are preventing everyone else from enjoying the obvious benefits of radiation. Please read the articles I have referenced, and see if you don't change your mind too.

References

1. Dixy Lee Ray, "Radiation Around Us," in *Rational Readings on Environmental Concerns*, ed. Jay H. Lehr, (New York, Van Nostrand Reinhold, 1992), 589

2. Dixy Lee Ray, "Radiation Around Us," in *Rational Readings on Environmental Concerns*, 590

3. "Three Mile Island," 927 Federal Supplement 834 (June 12, 1996), http://www.junkscience.com

4. Edward G. Remmers, "Nuclear Power: Putting the Risks Into Perspective," *Issues on the Environment*, (New York, American Council on Science and Health, 1992), 68

5. Mark M. Hart, "Radiation: What Is Important?", Handouts from a presentation at Lawrence Livermore National Laboratory, Livermore, California (May 2, 1998)

6. Cindy Cassady, "Radioactivity is Where the Public Least Expects" *Newsline*, (Livermore, California, Lawrence Livermore National Laboratory, August 5, 1994), 5

7. Petr Beckmann, *The Health Hazards of Not Going Nuclear*, (Boulder, Colorado, The Golem Press, (1985), 53

8. S.G. Hutchinson and F.I. Hutchinson, "Radioactivity in Everyday Life," *Journal of Chemical Education*, 74, (1997), 501

9. Rosalyn S. Yalow, "Radiation and Public Perception," in *Radiation and Public Perception: Benefits and Risks*, eds. Jack P. Young and Rosalyn S. Yalow, (Washington DC, American Chemical Society, 1995), 2

10. Joseph L. Bast, Peter J. Hill and Richard C. Rue, *Eco-Sanity*, (Lanham, Maryland, Madison Books, 1994), 104

11. Mehdi Sohrabi, "International Conference on High Levels of Natural Radiation, Held at Ramsar, Islamic Republic of Iran, 3-7 November 1990," *Nucl. Tracks Radiation Meas.*, 18, (1991), 357

12. Dixy Lee Ray, "Radiation Around Us," in *Rational Readings on Environmental Concerns*, 593

13. Masayoshi Yamamoto, Tsuneo Tsukatani and Yukio Katayama, "Residual Radioactivity in the Soil of the Semipalatinsk Nuclear Test Site in the Former USSR," *Health Physics*, 71, (1996), 142

14. Arthur B. Robinson, "Nuclear Wastelands?" *Access to Energy*, Cave Junction, Orgeon, (September 1996), 3

15. John R. Cameron, "Condensation of Laurie Taylor's 1980 Article," *Health Physics*, 73, (1997), 523

16. William R. Hendee, "Public Perception of Radiation Risks," in *Radiation and Public Perception: Benefits and Risks*, eds. Jack P. Young and Rosalyn S. Yalow, (Washington DC, American Chemical Society, 1995), 17

17. John Lenihan, *The Good News About Radiation*, (Madison, Wisconsin, Cogito Books, 1993), 138

18. Bernard L. Cohen, "The Hazards of Nuclear Power," in *The Resourceful Earth*, eds. Julian L. Simon and Herman Kahn, (Williston, Vermont, Basil Blackwell, 1984), 563

19. James Walsh, *True Odds*, (Santa Monica, California, Merritt Publishing, 1996), 14

20. Frank Furedi, *Culture of Fear*, (London, Cassell, 1997), 16

21. J.F. Diehl, "Achievements in food irradiation during the 20th century," *Nuclear News*, 44, (April 2000), 28

Chapter 21

Radiation Hormesis — A Little Means A Lot

Would you, could you, do you want to believe that exposure to low levels of radiation actually is good for you? Or, do you adhere to the premise that all radiation is harmful? It can be confusing because we have all been hammered with the simple equation of radiation = death. But, as we discussed in *Hormesis — Listen to Your Mother*, low doses of a substance can provide beneficial effects and high doses can be harmful.

If we think of radiation in terms of a linear model (all radiation is harmful), whenever we speak of radiation exposure, estimates for excess cancer deaths/sickness will be high. However, if we think of radiation in terms of the hormesis model, estimates will actually show fewer cancer deaths/sickness. For example, T.D. Luckey says the following: "Using a linear model, conservative estimates suggest the Chernobyl accident will cause 10,000 excess cancer deaths in the former U.S.S.R. within the next 70 years. In contrast, the hormesis model suggest that over 20,000 fewer cancer deaths will occur."[1]

Sound pie in the sky? It's not. There is overwhelming proof that the hormesis model of radiation exposure is sound, while the linear model is shaky at best.

Before atomic bombs were developed and used, radiobiologists accepted the biopositive effects of small doses of ionizing radiation. However, the holocausts at Hiroshima and Nagasaki mesmerized the world into accepting the thesis that "all doses of ionizing radiation are harmful."[2] This thesis continues to received media and monetary support after half a century. Yet, a report by Luckey contains **over 1,200 literature references** to studies on both animals and humans, confirming the beneficial effects of low level radiation. These include enhanced growth, improved reproductive capacity, improved immune responses, lower cancer rates, and longer lifespan.[3]

Let's look at some examples of the value of exposure to low levels of radiation.

- Japanese survivors of the attacks on Hiroshima and Nagasaki in 1945 who received low doses of radiation were compared with the population of Japan as a whole. The survivors had lower general mortality rates and lower cancer mortality. Exposed survivors are out-living the non-exposed population.[4]

- Workers at Los Alamos National Laboratory who were exposed to three times the amount of plutonium than the maximum currently recommended by the National Council on Radiation Protection have been studied for the past 50 years. Standard mortality ratios of the exposed workers when compared to the general population and to unexposed Los Alamos workers, were 0.43 and 0.77 respectively. This means that the number of exposed workers who have died as compared with these two groups is less by 57 percent and 23 percent. The second comparison is especially relevant, since it avoids variations due to differences in life style between Los Alamos workers and the general population.[5]

- A detailed epidemiological study found definitive reductions in lung cancer with increasing radon exposure. Bernard Cohen used this work to test the linear no-threshold theory for 1,601 U.S. counties. He reports: "With or without corrections for variations in smoking prevalence, there is a strong tendency for lung cancer rates to decrease with increasing radon exposure, in sharp contrast to the increase expected from the theory."[6]

- There is no evidence of increased mutation, genetic diseases, or cancer in animals or humans following exposure to low doses of ionizing radiation, even in Hiroshima and Nagasaki, in spite of extremely thorough and intensive investigations.[7]

So, what's the point of all this? Well, first, to let you know that not all radiation is bad, and the currently used linear no-threshold model is wrong. A large body of evidence shows conclusively that whole-body exposures to low doses of ionizing radiation reduces cancer mortality rates when compared with control populations in both experimental animals and humans. The decreased cancer incidence and mortality in animal experiments, in the nuclear industry, in army observers of atomic explosions, and in Japanese bomb victims is consistent.[8] The consistent results and the statistical significance of much of the data from human experience and animal experiments destroy two myths: 1 - all radiation is harmful, and 2 - the linear model is valid for low doses of ionizing radiation. All of this flies in the face of what you have heard. The facts, as they say, speak for themselves. Now to my second point.

Since the linear model is being used (contrary to science), billions and billions of dollars have been spent (and will continue to be) based on a factually incorrect thesis. Klaus Becker says: "Ten thousands of millions of dollars are spent every year worldwide in decommissioning, remediation, or nuclear waste programs, which could obviously be used much more beneficially in other areas of public and individual health, in rich, and even more so in poor countries of the world."[9] Misuse of the linear no-threshold model portends spending in excess of $1 trillion in the United States alone for negligible health benefits just for government environmental cleanup programs, while truly significant public health protections are unfunded.[4]

The pattern of using a disproven (or at least highly questionable) theory as the foundation for law and regulation continues, resulting in the throwing away of dollars that could be better used elsewhere. The linear no-threshold model is wrong, and we need to junk it. Radiation, it's just not what you think it is.

References

1.   T.D. Luckey, *Radiation Hormesis*, (Boca Raton, Florida, CRC Press, 1991), 98

2.   T.D. Luckey, *Radiation Hormesis*, 177

3.   T.D. Luckey, *Radiation Hormesis*, 53

4.   Jim Muckerheide, "The health effects of low-level radiation: Science, data, and corrective action," *Nuclear News*, 38, (September 1995), 26

5.   George L. Voelz, J.N.P. Lawrence and E.R. Johnson, "Fifty Years of Plutonium Exposure to the Manhattan Project Plutonium Workers," *Health Physics*, 73, (1997), 611

6.   Bernard L. Cohen, "Test of the linear-no threshold theory of radiation car-
     cinogenesis for inhaled radon decay products," *Health Physics*, 68, (1995),
     157

7.   Petr Beckmann, *The Health Hazards of Not Going Nuclear*, (Boulder, Colo-
     rado, The Golem Press, 1985), 59

8.   T.D. Luckey, *Radiation Hormesis*, 176

9.   Klaus Becker, "Low-Dose Cost/Benefit Assessment - A View from Europe,"
     Health Physics, 74, (1998), 267

Chapter 22

Cancer Clusters — Shoot First, Ask Nothing

How do we decide a cancer cluster exists? Let's look at a hypothetical situation. Assume that you have been diagnosed with cancer. You realize that around your neighborhood, five out of the six of your closest neighbors have at least one person in the household with cancer. You ask: Isn't this more than the expected number of cases for my neighborhood? Then one day you look outside and see the power pole on the street and connect this with a report you vaguely remember about electromagnetic fields and cancer. Suddenly, you are convinced you must be part of a cancer cluster. In most cases, this is just not true as one out of every three people in the U.S. will develop cancer sometime during his or her life. Statistically, cancer clusters are anomalies, and are headline grabbers or ways for protestors to make their point against things like hazardous waste sites or electromagnetic fields.

Let's look at some of the cases of "false" clusters, as well as "true" clusters and their causes, then we'll examine the statistics behind diagnosing clusters.

A study of a site in Woburn, Massachussets that was reported as a cancer cluster found that the 20 childhood leukemia cases in the area was simply an anomaly. Since the water supply (wells) in Woburn contained traces of trichloroethylene, this was immediately blamed as the cause. However, none of the contaminants found in Woburn, including the trichloroethylene, are causes of leukemia.[1] Bruce Ames and his colleagues in their HERP Index, report the following to be more carcinogenic than a glass of tap water from the Woburn wells found to contain trichloroethylene: one glass of herbal tea; one non-poisonous raw mushroom; one can of diet soda; one cup of coffee; one glass of wine or beer.[2]

Another example is what was reported as an "epidemic" of male breast cancer among telephone linemen in New York State. A close look at the data reveals that although a relative risk of 6.5 to 1 was obtained, only two cases were actually recorded. Furthermore, the two people involved were not even linemen, but phone company office workers. Yet, on the basis of these two cases, some scientists and many media outlets concluded incorrectly that there was a serious problem.[3]

Because most cancer clusters happen by chance, health officials are usually reluctant to investigate reports of localized excess in cancer rates. The Centers for Disease Control and Prevention gave up routinely investigating cancer clusters because of the intensive resources required for the little information that was gained.[4] However, it should be noted that on some occasions investigations of cancer clusters have proven fruitful. Typically, these have been occupational or medical clusters and not neighborhood clusters.

One study of lung cancer among packaging industry workers revealed that polyvinyl chlorides were the cause. Another study of vaginal cancer in young women identified diethylstilbestrol as the cause.[5] These two industry-related cases are important because the disease was rare and suddenly increased in frequency.

Raymond R. Neutra, California Department of Health Services, reports that only one carcinogen has ever been discovered as the result of a neighborhood cluster. Death certificates showed 20 mesothelioma deaths (which is uniquely associated with fibrous minerals) in four years in a Turkish village with a population of 800. Investigation revealed that the culprit was the mineral *erionite* which was found in plentiful supply in the soil and building materials of the village.[6]

Now, let's look at cancer. As mentioned in the beginning of the chapter, one out of every three people in the United States will develop cancer at some point during their lives. This is called the background risk or "natural" rate of cancer and it is ours by virtue of our birth. If you analyze cancer rates geographically by state, county, city, or neighborhood, you will likely find that some areas will have a cancer rate of exactly 1 in 3. However, most areas have cancer rates that are greater or less than 1 in 3.[7] Jane Orient reports: "Some clusters don't have a common cause; they just happen. It is not necessarily abnormal for a neighborhood to have 'higher than average' incidence of a particular disease just as it's normal for some students to have a higher than average score on a test."[8]

Lori Miller Kase says: "According to Raymond R. Neutra, probability theory suggests that 17% of the 29,000 towns or census tracts in the U.S. will have at least one of the 80 recognized types of cancer elevated in any given decade, producing 4,930 chance clusters."[9] Neutra also points out that the incidence of a particular cancer in a neighborhood needs to be more than eight times the normal rate to achieve statistical significance as a cluster. In other words, you need to find eight times as many cases as you would expect, and there has to be a specific type of cancer involved.

Here's a good example of a case that has the parameters necessary for an investigation. Please note that this is a case of a "medical cluster" not a cancer cluster.

In comparing public health response to a noticeably obvious medical cluster with a cancer cluster, Neutra used the interesting case of the eleven blue men. This is described in detail by Berton Roueche in his book *The Medical Detectives.*[10] In 1944 eleven very ill or unconscious derelicts were found in a neighborhood of New York City. All of them had turned an unusual sky blue color. The diagnosis on the first to arrive was cyanosis, which is a result of an insufficient supply of oxygen in the blood. The doctor postulated that this was a case of carbon monoxide poisoning. Within a few hours, ten more blue men were brought in with similar symptoms and in a state of shock. However, the symptoms were not quite right for gas poisoning since the headaches and general dopiness normally associated with gas were missing. This led the medical investigators to look elsewhere for the cause. It turns out the men were the victims of a poisoning so rare that only ten previous outbreaks of it had been recorded in the medical literature. They had contracted methemoglobinemia, which is caused by ingesting sodium nitrite. Investigation implicated a certain restaurant and the use of salt. It was discovered that one of the restaurant's salt shakers contained sodium nitrite instead of sodium chloride. The victims had eaten oatmeal that had been flavored with sodium nitrite instead of salt. After cooking, it was estimated that the proportion of nitrite in each batch of oatmeal was about 1 to 80. This is considerably higher than the 1 part per 5,000 allowed when sodium nitrite is used to prevent the growth of deadly botulism agents.[10]

Now, how were the procedures in this case different from the procedures used to investigate a cancer cluster? First, there was no question that the complaint was legitimate. All eleven men were sky blue in color, and how many sky blue people have you ever seen? Contrast this with how many people you know who have cancer.

Another cluster involved six patients who developed muscle pain after eating fried fish. Investigation by health authorities identified the condition as Haff Disease, which is caused by a toxin sometimes present in buffalo fish. Four of the cases were traced to a single Louisiana wholesaler.[11]

As Neutra points out: "With cancer clusters things are usually much less clear-cut, and an experienced public health worker finds that a majority of calls can be legitimately handled with verbal or written explanations about the epidemiology of cancer."[6] Secondly, cancer has a long and indefinite incubation period. In the cases of the eleven blue men or victims of infectious disease, the relevant exposure occurred in the very recent past. The same analysis applies to those who ate the buffalo fish. These exposures are very easy to pinpoint and connect with the illness. But with cancer the exposure could have occurred many years ago, making it difficult to remember and reconstruct the details.

If neighborhood cancer clusters are so rare, why do we see so many? One answer is that the media and concerned citizens bring them to our attention. Couple this with the fact that as Atul Gawande states, we're programmed to see clusters, since people assume that the pattern of a large population will be replicated in all its subjects. This type of thinking has been called the Belief in the Law of Small Numbers. It is just like assuming that after seeing a long sequence of red on the roulette wheel, we feel that 'black' is due. We assume that a sequence of R-R-R-R-R is somehow less random than, say, R-R-B-R-B. But, the two sequences are equally likely.[11]

Although several carcinogens have been discovered through occupational or medical clusters, only one neighborhood cancer cluster has ever been traced to an environmental cause. So the next time you read or hear about a neighborhood cancer cluster supposedly caused by a power transformer or chemical, pause and give thought to some of the statistics on cancer. Unlike an outbreak of infectious disease, which can be linked to a well defined recent exposure, a cluster of cancer cases might have its root in an exposure that occurred 10 to 20 years ago. Or it might just be a statistical anomaly because of the high incidence of cancer in our world.

References

1. Steven Milloy, *Science Without Sense*, (Washington, D.C., The Cato Institute, 1995), 26

2. Bruce N. Ames, Renae Magaw and Lois Swirsky Gold, "Ranking Possible Carcinogenic Hazards," *Science*, 236, (April 17, 1987), 271

3. James Walsh, *True Odds*, (Santa Monica, California, Merritt Publishing, 1996), 128

4. Lori Miller Kase, "Why Community Cancer Clusters Are Often Ignored," *Scientific American*, 275 (September, 1996), 85

5. Chris Raymond, "Nagging Doubt, Public Opinion Offer Obstacles to Ending 'Cluster' Studies," *Journal of the American Medical Association*, 261, (April 28, 1989), 2297

6. Raymond R. Neutra, "Counterpoint from a Cluster," *American Journal of Epidemiology*, 132, (July, 1990), 1

7. Steven Milloy, *Science Without Sense*, 26

8. Jane M. Orient, in *Rational Readings on Environmental Concerns*, ed. Jay H. Lehr, (New York, Van Nostrand Reinhold, 1992), 189

9. Lori Miller Kase, "Why Community Cancer Clusters Are Often Ignored," 85

10. Berton Roueche, *The Medical Detectives*, (New York, Washignton Square Press, 1982), 1

11. Atul Gawande, "The Cancer-Cluster Myth," *The New Yorker*, (February 8, 1999), 34

Chapter 23

Poverty is the Worst Carcinogen

What environmental problems kill humans in the greatest numbers today? It isn't Alar, ozone depletion, dioxins, nuclear waste, electromagnetic radiation, pesticide residue, PCBs or asbestos. What kills the most people is dung smoke and diarrhea, which are both directly related to poverty. Poverty can therefore be described as the worst carcinogen. Or, as Alan Moghissi states: "Poverty is the equivalent to exposure to the most toxic pollutant."[1]

Does it surprise you that diarrhea is a culprit? It shouldn't. According to UNICEF, 3.8 million children in the Third World under the age of five died in 1993 from from diarrheal diseases caused by impure drinking water. As Gregg Easterbrook points out: "In the First World, death from diarrhea is about as common as comet strikes; in the developing world diarrhea kills far more people than cancer. Most of Africa, the Indian subcontinent, and Latin America have no wastewater treatment facilities. Yet Western public consciousness continues to focus on exotic ecological threats while ignoring millions of annual deaths from basic environmental problems of water and air."[2] According to another UNICEF report published in 1997, almost three billion people (about half the world's population) live without clean toilets. "More than two million children die each year...infected by bacteria that could easily have been avoided if they had been flushed down a pipe."[3]

Impure drinking water and waste treatment are not the only killers. When children die in the Third World, it's mainly because they live in poorly ventilated huts where fuel wood, cow dung, or agricultural wastes are used for heating and cooking. Gurindhir Shahi, an official of the United Nations Development Program says: "Smoke inside a hut like this can be unbelievable. Women and children, who spend most time in the home, are most harmed. Today 40% of the global population heats and cooks with biomass in raw form."[4] This type of indoor air pollution was covered in Chapter 2: The Good Old Days.

Basic pollution in the Third World is far more significant than all First World ecological problems combined. Easterbrook quotes Eric Chivian, a psychiatrist on the faculty at Harvard Medical School who started an organization called the Project on Global Environmental Change and Health: "I've had great difficulty interesting environmental organizations in human health in poor countries. They want to talk about forest loss and species diversity in the developing world but have much less interest in human health there. Nobody should kid themselves that they are doing Bangladesh a favor when they worry about global warming."[5]

It strikes me funny (ironic, not ha-ha) that environmental organizations constantly throw themselves at the cause of pollution here in the United States, rail about some part per zillion pollutant in dirt that a child might eat, and seem more worried about trees, animals, and pretty places in the Third World than they are about millions of children dying each year due to simple pollution problems that are eminently solvable.

At the 1992 United Conference on Economic Development held in Rio di Janeiro environmentalists from the northern hemisphere staged demonstrations every day. One *Journal do Brazil* headline said: "Americans and Europeans March in Defense of Animals, Forests, and Ecology." The subhead told the real story though: "Brazilians protest hunger, poverty, and oppression."[6]

Dixy Lee Ray and Lou Guzzo quote Dr. Norman Borlaug, a Nobel Prize recipient who is considered one of the fathers of the Green Revolution: "I am concerned that the growing anti-science and anti-technology bias in affluent countries will adversely affect the prospects for agricultural development. In effect, the (haves) are telling the (have-nots) that they should stay with current simple lifestyles since great material well-being isn't what it is made out to be. How many people in the First World would be willing to cut their life spans by one half, see up to half their children die before reaching the age of 10, often as a result of minor and easily curable illness, live in illiteracy with substandard shelter, clothing and sanitation, and face bleak prospects of no improvement in economic well being for themselves or their children? Unwittingly, this is the continuing fate that the affluent anti-technology groups are wishing for the Third World's people."[7]

In referencing "anti-technology groups," Borlaug is referring to those who believe that economic growth spurred by technology is destroying the environment. Borlaug also makes an important point that the wealthy are more concerned about the environment than the poor. This is pretty simple in my mind. When you are worried about day-to-day survival, there is little or no time to worry about ecology. If you're hungry, not much else matters.

It has been shown that more than 2 million children die (5 million total persons) per year in the Third World from diseases that cause diarrhea. Countless others die from indoor air pollution because smoke from fires used to heat and cook contain dangerous levels of pollutants. These conditions exist because of abject destitution, making poverty the worst carcinogen. We spend billions of dollars here and worldwide making sure that the environment is safe, to ensure that species are protected, yet we seem to ignore the human factor. As Whitney Young, former Urban League President stated: "The war on pollution is one that should be waged after the war on poverty."[8]

References

1. A. Alan Moghissi, "Poverty, Ignorance, and the Environment: The Three Challenges of the 21st Century," *Environment International*, 24, (1998), 379

2. Gregg Easterbrook, *A Moment on Earth*, (New York, Viking, 1995), 579

3. Kathryn Brown, "Not a Pretty Picture," *Discover*, 18, (January 1998), 104

4. Gregg Easterbrook, *A Moment on Earth*, (New York, Viking, 1995), 578

5. Gregg Easterbrook, *A Moment on Earth*, (New York, Viking, 1995), 580

6. Mark Dowie, *Losing Ground*, (Cambridge, Massachusetts, MIT Press, 1997), 167

7. Dixy Lee Ray and Lou Guzzo, *Environmental Overkill: Whatever Happened to Common Sense?*, (Washington, D.C., Regnery Gateway, 1993), 68

8. Whitney Young, quoted in Mark Dowie, *Losing Ground*, (Cambridge, Massachusetts, MIT Press, 1997), 25

Section 6:

The Culture of the Environment

Chapter 24

Environmental Indicators — "Gimme the Bad News Doc!"

So you think that our environment continues to deteriorate? Of course you do. You have not heard otherwise. Let's go over what most Americans believe to be the current state of the environment in America, focusing on air and water quality. Then, we'll go over **what is really happening**, that no one seems to want to tell you.

One poll after another shows that the citizens of the United States are unaware of improvements in environmental issues. In a Wirthlin Group 1993 poll, 75 percent of those contacted believed that problems regarding pollution and the environment would get significantly worse during their lifetimes.[1] A 1997 poll conducted by Hamilton & Staff showed that 58 percent believed air quality had gotten worse over the past ten years.[2] A Gallup Poll conducted in 1990 revealed that only 14 percent of Americans believed that the United States had made a "great deal of progress" on the environment. By 1999 this figure had risen to 36 percent.[3] But that still leaves about two-thirds of the public unconvinced about environmental improvement.

A good portion of the blame lies with the media coverage that concentrates on issues like Alar, the preservative used by apple growers that 60 Minutes portrayed as a threat to children (the risk was grossly exaggerated), oil spills, tainted Perrier water, etc. Even the younger generation is convinced we are in deep trouble. Arthur Robinson provides the following, "The Nuclear Energy Institute in Washington, D.C. reported that a freshman at Eagle Rock Junior High in Idaho urged classmates to sign a petition demanding strict control or total elimination of the chemical "dihydrogen monoxide," which causes excessive sweating and vomiting; is a major component in acid rain;

can cause severe burns when in the gaseous state; can cause death when accidentally inhaled; contributes to erosion; decreases the effectiveness of automobile brakes and has been found in the tumors of terminal cancer patients. A total of 50 students were asked if they supported a ban on the chemical; 43 said yes, 6 were undecided, and only 1 knew that the chemical was water. Even though 98 percent of the students did not seem to have an understanding of basic chemical nomenclature, 86 percent believed it was their right to support this restriction of technological freedom."[4] James Glassman suggests that if the same experiment was tried on adults, at least as many would support the ban on water.[5] This type of thinking is all too pervasive with environmental issues.

Before I point out the facts on air and water quality, I want to make an important point. While bad news receives heavy coverage, important information about the environment is either underreported, or outright ignored. For example, when San Francisco met the Federal Ozone Standard in 1992, the San Francisco Chronicle reported the news on page 16.[1] West coast or east coast, the media treatment is the same. In his book, *A Moment on Earth*, journalist Gregg Easterbrook recounts his surprise at his finding on page A24 of the New York Times a short news account under the headline "Air Found Cleaner in U.S. Cities." Such treatment, he said, "suggested that the world was somehow disappointed by an inappropriately encouraging discovery."[6]

As promised, the news is good. There have been great improvements in air and water quality, and they follow. You won't see these in the paper, or hear about them on 60 Minutes. We'll discuss air quality first.

Since the passing of the Clean Air Act in 1970, aggregate emissions of the six "criteria" pollutants (carbon monoxide, particulates, volatile organic compounds, sulfur dioxide, nitrogen dioxide, and lead) have fallen by up to 64 percent.[7]

A recent comprehensive report by the Pacific Research Institute disputes popular perception, finding significant declines in air pollution, water pollution, and toxic chemicals in the environment. The authors, Steven Hayward and Julie Majeres state: "The improvement in air quality is perhaps the single greatest environmental success of the last generation, and is arguably the largest public success story in recent U.S. history." The table below lists the percentage changes in ambient air quality for the six pollutants regulated under the Clean Air Act between 1976 and 1998.[7]

Table 24.1 - Air Emission Changes Between 1976 and 1998[a]

Pollutant	Change, % drop
Sulfur Dioxide	64.7
Nitrogen Dioxide	37.9
Ozone	27.6
Carbon Monoxide	67.2
Lead	97.3
Particulates (PM 10)*	26.4

*From 1988 to 1998
(a) Steven Hayward and Julie Majeres, "Index of Leading Environmental Indicators," Sixth Edition, (San Francisco, Pacific Research Insitute, April 2001)

Water quality in the United States has also improved to a point that should be trumpeted by the press as an unprecedented success story. But, since they will not, here are the facts.

By the end of the millennium, the United States spent more than a trillion ($1,000,000,000,000) dollars on behalf of water quality since the passage of the Clean Water Act.[1] There is little doubt that the water quality has much improved since the first Earth Day of 1970. Gregg Easterbrook says, "In the Western world water quality is the most successful of first generation environmental initiatives," and provides some of the following examples.

In the early 1970s, the Great Lakes, Puget Sound, Chesapeake Bay, the Saint Lawrence Seaway, the harbors of Boston, New York, and San Diego, the Charles and the Potomac and other water bodies in the United States and Western Europe were pronounced "dead" or facing mortality. Today, these water bodies are biologically vibrant and showing annual improvement."

"As of 1992 all sewage generated in the United States is treated before discharging, usually in facilities that bring the water to a standard safe for swimming."

"Statistics kept by the National Oceanographic and Atmospheric Administration (NOAA) show declining levels of most contaminants along both U.S. coastlines since the early 1970s."[8]

One of the best examples is the Great Lakes. There have been large improvements in water quality and wildlife health in and around the Great Lakes over the past 30 years.[7] Hayward and Majeres report, "The Great Lakes are a phenomenal success story in reducing persistent, bioaccumulative toxics. The most significant threat to the ecological balance of the Great Lakes no longer comes mainly from industrial pollution or toxics, but from biological imbalances. The proliferation of zebra mussels, a nonnative species that has entered the Great Lakes region chiefly in the ballast of water of cargo ships, currently presents one of the most significant environmental challenges for these water bodies. The zebra mussel is only one of 130 nonnative or "exotic" species now found in the Great Lakes. These exotic species crowd out habitat of other indigenous species in the lakes. Yet, the Great Lakes Initiative and many environmental activists continue their crusade against chlorine and other synthetic chemicals that no longer pose a serious threat."[7] Hayward and Majeres quote Professor Bill Cooper of Michigan State University: "If one wished to allocate scarce monetary and human resources so as to maximize the reduction in ecological risk per unit of resource expended, one would do more good by regulating and/or limiting the introduction of exotics than by obtaining marginal reductions in trace levels of existing toxicants."[7] Suffice to say, environmental groups concerned with the Great Lakes are chasing the wrong rabbit here. The introduction and proliferation of alien/exotic species in the Great Lakes is by far more damaging to these massive ecosystems than any remaining chemical pollutants.

The strides we have made in improving our air and water quality in the United States are staggering. The most polluted day in Los Angeles is better than an average or even a good day 27 years ago in most of the country's industrial cities.[9] The environment is cleaner and safer than at any time in the past 50 years. The average American today is exposed to fewer potentially harmful pollutants than at any time since the 1930s. Air and water pollution, which had risen during the 1940s and 1950s, have fallen constantly and considerably since that time. You just never heard about it because the media is so focused on the "If it bleeds, it leads" paradigm. I have yet to see any good news about the environment as a headline. The awesome positive changes we have made as a nation are buried in the deepest sections of our newspapers and rarely, if ever, broadcast on TV or radio.

Just as a postscript, here's a pollution paradox from Larry Laudan in his book *Danger Ahead*. "All of us have read about how the depletion in the ozone layer threatens to dramatically increase the frequency of skin cancers. What is less known is that, along with the ozone layer, one of the major filters of cancer causing ultraviolet radiation is air pollution. Accordingly, as we clean up the air in our cities, we inadvertently increase UV exposure levels, just as surely (and probably more dramatically than) ozone holes in the upper atmosphere do."[10] But don't worry. The predicted 5% decrease in ozone will affect you as much as if you moved 70 miles closer to the equator.[11]

References

1. B. DeWeil, S. Hayward, L. Jones and M.D. Smith, "Index of Leading Environmental Indicators," (San Francisco, Pacific Research Institute, April 1997)

2. Linda Raber, "Public unaware of air quality gains," *Chemical & Engineering News*, 97 (May 26, 1997), 26

3. Bjorn Lomborg, *The Skeptical Environmentalist*, (Cambridge, United Kingdom, Cambridge University Press, 2001), 215

4. Arthur B. Robinson, *Access to Energy*, (Cave Junction, Oregon, Vol. 25, November 1997)

5. James S. Glassman, "Dihydrogen Monoxide: Unrecognized Killer," *The Washington Post* (1997)

6. Gregg Easterbrook, *A Moment on Earth*, (New York, Viking, 1995), xiii

7. Steven Hayward and Julie Majeres, "Index of Leading Environmental Indicators," Sixth Edition, (San Francisco, Pacific Research Institute, April 2001)

8. Gregg Easterbrook, *A Moment on Earth*, (New York, Viking, 1995), 628

9. Paul R. Portney, "Counting the cost: The growing role of economics in environmental decisionmaking," *Environment*, 40, (March 1998), 14

10. Larry Laudan, *Danger Ahead: The Risks You Really Face on Life's Highway*, (New York, John Wiley & Sons, 1997), 158

11. Hugh W. Ellsaesser, "The Ozone Layer," in *Standard Handbook of Environmental Science, Health and Technology*, eds. Jay H. Lehr and Janet K. Lehr, (New York, McGraw-Hill, 2000), 20.33

Chapter 25

Bad News is Big News

Often the media get too excited by environmental stories and end up blowing them out of proportion. What is happening is all too clear. The media once prided themselves on truth and accuracy but now flourish on lies, half-truths, and illusions about environmental poisons. In an effort to be first on a topic, news outlets do not take time to really research the issues, and the result is unbalanced coverage.

As people watch continued coverage about the latest environmental scare, they can hardly be blamed for concluding that one part per billion of some chemical is much worse than cigarettes or alcohol (two of the leading killers). It is no secret that apocalypse sells: nuclear accidents, asbestos, pesticides, Love Canal, Times Beach, the greenhouse effect, the ozone hole.[1] In an internal memo, the EPA admitted that its priorities in regulating carcinogens are based more on public opinion (as formed by the media) than on their own estimate of the risks.[2]

In a recent poll by the Pew Research Center for the People & the Press, four in ten journalists said they purposely avoided newsworthy stories to benefit the interests of their own news organizations. The biggest cause of this is market pressure that causes news organizations to avoid stories considered too boring or complicated.[3]

Make no mistake about it, science is losing its constituency, most of which now count on the media to do the research and report the results. A majority of Americans still tell pollsters they believe in science, but in many cases the so called science they advocate includes astrology, yoga, and ESP.[1] Margaretha Isaacson, the South African physician and hemorrhagic fever specialist who stopped the transmission of Ebola virus at Ngaliema Hospital in Kinshasa during the original 1976 outbreak commented on how ignorance helps feed the public's sense of terror:

"Ebola is of absolutely no danger to the world at large. It is a dangerous virus, but it's relatively rare and quite easily contained. The virus needs the right conditions to multiply, whatever the virus is, be it Ebola or plague. It's not enough to just have the accident. The virus must first find itself in a favorable environment before it can affect anyone. The media is scaring the world out of its wits, and movies like *Outbreak* are doing people a great disservice."[4]

The average reporter works toward two goals because the typical daily newspaper cares about two things. The first is making deadlines; the second is being interesting. Accuracy is not high up in the hierarchy.[5] In fact, accuracy slows one down tremendously. It means getting confirmations and doing research, as opposed to calling a few experts and quoting their opinions. And these days, there are plenty of "experts" with their own particular environmental agendas who are willing to comment on the latest scare of the month. Speaking of experts, how about Meryl Streep speaking as an expert on Alar before Congress? I was unaware of her credentials as a chemical engineer. Or what about a congressional committee inviting Jessica Lange, Sissy Spacek and Jane Fonda to testify on farm problems because they all had starred in movies concerning farms?[6]

The standards of evidence and the rules of publication are very different in the worlds of science and journalism. Because of this when journalists cover scientific topics, solid communication does not always take place, and the resulting stories are at times misleading. News organizations seem to tolerate sloppiness more than ever. Reporters usually are not even upset if they get a fact wrong. You might get a retraction, but an error in a front page story is not properly corrected by a retraction on page A18. People remember the original article and it's the impression that is going to last.

Alan Simpson, former Senator from Wyoming, points out that journalists have no governing body that oversees their work and punishes them for sins and mistakes (like scientists). Unlike other professions or crafts that rely on a high degree of public trust, journalism has no reasonable method for measuring performance. There are no procedures for evaluating credibility and honesty, and no periodic testing and certification. Simpson also suggests that instead of using the five W's (who, what, when, where, and why), the profession is more interested on the five C's (conflict, controversy, cleverness, lack of clarity, and the fifth C is for television people who must always have their hair carefully coiffed.)[7]

A study examining changing environmental values in the nations' press compared views of newspaper editors in 1977 with those in 1992.[8] Key items discussed include:

- With the end of the Cold War, the environment may replace East-West confrontation as the key threat facing humanity.
- By far the biggest problem most editors face in reporting environmental stories is the sheer enormity and complexity of the subjects.
- Nearly 70% of the editors endorsed the slogan of the old Chicago Times: "The duty of a newspaper is to print the news and raise hell."

The last statement gives credence to Ben Wattenberg's comments that news judgements are often based on three criteria:

1. Bad news is big news.
2. Good news is no news.
3. Good news is bad news.[9]

Controversy sells, and journalists and the publications they work for do not prosper by simply detailing the mundane facts associated with good news. Dorothy Nelkin reports that when covering environmental and health issues, "Journalistic norms lead reporters to adopt a polarized approach to the problem, emphasizing conflict rather than knowledge, and this results in reporting of evidence that is often inconsistent and confused." She says that some of the problem stems from needing to respond to fast breaking events, with technical uncertainty, and conflicting information. Also, the necessity of being "first" with a story emphasizes the time issue. "Time is nearly always of the essence in reporting," and many times reporters lack the time to deal adequately with the uncertainties inherent in environmental disputes.[10]

As Michael Fumento also notes: "Journalists will often eschew reading a science or medical magazine article, in favor of simply reading the abstract." He cites a study on AIDS virus infections on college campuses. Some reporters declared it was a new study that showed an "alarming increase" in infections over those reported in an older study. This was, in fact, the old study, which had been held from publication for 18 months. The original article definitely made the date clear, but it was absent from the abstract, so some of the news outlets missed it. The "alarming increase" shows the ability of the media to find something alarming and new in absolutely nothing.[5] Dean Edell observes that wire services provide most of the information we receive: "I have never in my twenty-year career seen a reporter first look for and then read the original medical journal report or research project on which a health story is based."[11]

In their search for attention-grabbing news, newspaper and television reporters not only single out weak studies; they may focus on the one positive result in a sea of negative data (in the case of poisons, the one bad apple in the barrel). Charles Mann reports: "This was the case with coverage of two big studies on occupational exposure to electromagnetic fields (EMF) that appeared in the *American Journal of Epidemiology*. The first study of 223,000 French and Canadian electric utility workers found no link between EMF and 25 of the 27 varieties of cancer in the study; the exception, two rare types of leukemia, had a weak and inconsistent positive association with EMF. Yet, the *Wall Street Journal* reported the study under the headline, 'Magnetic Fields Linked to Leukemia'." In 1995, the *American Journal of Epidemiology* published the second study on 139,000 workers at five U.S. utilities. No association was found between exposure to EMF and 17 of 18 types of cancer, including the leukemias barely linked to EMF by the first study. The sole exceptions were eye and brain cancers – conditions that showed no link to EMF in the first study. However, the headline of the *Wall Street Journal* article that reported the second study was "Link Between EMF, Brain Cancer is Suggested by Study at 5 Utilities."[12]

Mann quotes Jerry Bishop, who wrote on the *Wall Street Journal* articles. "People are not interested in what disease (a risk factor) doesn't cause, but what it might cause. We've had this argument with scientists many times over the past few years." Lawrence Altman, reporter for *Times* is also quoted by Mann. "If there is a blame for such coverage, much of it belongs to scientific journals. The *Journal of the National Cancer Institute* sent out a big release touting a study on breast cancer as if it were the biggest thing since whatever. I don't recall them telling us that it was only one of 40 studies and probably had little meaning." Along these lines, Ross Prentice of the University of Washington says: "Journalists do overemphasize individual studies, but they are often invited to do that by medical journals. I've seen some of the press releases that journals and universities send to journalists. It's a wonder sometimes that the reporting is as good as it is."[12]

Headlines can also be misleading and not accurately reflect the stories under them. The following was reported by John Paulos: "Although their stories, reported on the same events and appeared on the same day, the *New York Times* and *Wall Street Journal* headlined them, respectively, 'Meeting lays bare the abyss between AIDS and its cure,' and 'Scientists have an optimistic outlook about the prospect in AIDS research.'"[13]

An interesting bit of reporting occurred in my hometown of Livermore, California a few years back. The local newspaper ran a headline on the front page, "Report Raps Lab Over Radiation Exposure," while alongside this, a much smaller headline read, "Man Buried in Gravel Plant Hopper." The large headline introduced a three-column article, continued on another page. It discussed a 60 page report detailing how three Lawrence Livermore National Laboratory (LLNL) workers were accidentally exposed to X-rays during an experiment. The report said, "at least 16 management procedures at LLNL were either less than adequate or inherently weak." The three individuals, according to a medical evaluation, were not expected to develop any disabilities due to the exposure. By contrast, the one-column article with the smaller headline reported on a man who was killed when he slipped into a gravel hopper and was buried alive. No detail on inadequate safety procedures or oversight committees was included.

Importantly, the blame lies not only with the media, but with the scientific community. As Edith Efron says in her excellent book, *The Apocalyptics*, which discusses how environmental politics controls what we know about cancer: "The inadequacy of the coverage is the inadequacy of the informants. Much of the blame lies on the scientific community that did not speak up, as well as those who did speak, but with forked tongues." She emphatically states that she cannot indict the lay press for failing to understand what it takes years to understand. To write her 500 page book, she read about 10,000 papers on carcinogenesis and genetics and about 500 books. To write the epilogue alone, she had to read histories of cancer epidemiology, several epidemiology textbooks and some 5,000 additional papers in that field. She points out: "Reporters must write swiftly; they cover the daily news. They could not take off several years to do their 'homework.' Indeed, as laymen, they have never realized how much homework there was to do."[14] Also, scientists, who are usually writing for their peers, write in such a convoluted and confusing manner, that very few people can understand what they are saying.

As mentioned earlier, the media adheres pretty strictly to the idea that good news is bad news or no news at all. This reads out to be that the media is biased against negative studies. A negative study is one that produces negative results. That is, it does not find any association between the two things being studied. For example, it finds no evidence that Chemical X causes cancer. A positive study produces positive results: it *does* find evidence that Chemical X causes cancer. This is consistent then with the idea that bad news is good news. Gideon Koren and Naomi Klein compared the coverage that newspapers gave to two studies, one negative and one positive, published back-to-back in the March 20, 1991 issues of the *Journal of the American Medical Association* (JAMA). Both studies analyzed an area of public health concern; radiation as a risk for cancer.[15] A positive study by Steve Wing et. al. showed a mean 63% increase in risk for leukemia in white men working at the Oak Ridge National Laboratory (ORNL).[16] A negative study by Seymour Jablon et. al. failed to show an increased risk of cancer in people residing near nuclear facilities.[17] The Wing study involved 8,318 white men hired at ORNL between 1943 and 1972. Results revealed a relatively low mortality compared with U.S. white men except for leukemia, which was 63% higher. By contrast, the Jablon study covered over 900,000 cancer deaths from 1950 through 1984 in 197 counties with or near nuclear installations. The results indicated that deaths due to leukemia were not more frequent in the study group than in the general population.

Koren and Kelin searched 168 newspapers identified via seven online databases. They found 17 newspapers that published 19 reports on at least one of the two studies. Here's what they found:

- 10 reports covered both stories
- 9 reports were dedicated only to the positive story
- 0 reports were dedicated only to the negative story.

In reports covering both studies, the portions of the articles dealing with the positive results (the bad news) were significantly longer than the portions dealing with the negative (median number of words was 345 vs. 122 words). Of the 10 reports that covered both stories, eight headlines described the positive study and only two described the negative study.[15]

To review: the papers appeared back-to-back with the negative study first. Both were the same length (six pages). Both were included in an AMA news release, so it is unlikely that journalists would miss one of them more than the other. The negative study (the good news) covered 900,000 people, the positive study slightly more than 8,000, yet the positive study (an increase in cancer and leukemia deaths) got much more press and headline space.

I should note, however, that the two articles, like most technical articles, were written for the scientific community and therefore, were difficult to understand because of their stiff writing and specialized jargon. I can easily see why a reporter would read an abstract rather than an entire article. I was not able to get a copy of JAMA's news release, so I cannot speak to its clarity or lack thereof.

Here's another example of bias in reporting results. Social worker William Epstein wrote two versions of an article summarizing fictitious research. He described how social workers attempted to relieve the symptoms of a child suffering from asthma by separating him temporarily from his parents. Epstein sent a version of the article in which the social workers' intervention benefited the child to 70 scholarly journals and the other, in which the intervention failed, to another 70. Fifty-three percent of the journals receiving the positive version of the paper accepted it, compared with only 14% of those that were sent the negative version. He concluded that his paper's reviewers were biased by their preferences, since they approved of a paper confirming the efficacy of social work and disapproved of one questioning it. They held this bias in spite of the fact that either conclusion was equally significant and the papers were otherwise methodologically identical.[18]

It is also evident within the scientific community that getting something reported builds support among those that fund research. Unfortunately, finding bad news is much more popular. Gary Taubes quotes one National Institute of Environmental Health Sciences researcher who asked for anonymity: "Investigators who find an effect get support, and investigators who don't find an effect don't get support. When times are tough it becomes extremely difficult for investigators to be objective."[19]

This issue alone is enough to fill an entire book, and is certainly one of the reasons why I chose to write this particular book. There will be much more to follow surrounding this topic in the next few chapters as we continue our investigation. The main point here is that there are forces combining to ensure that the environmental information you see in the media is often half-truths, outright lies, or simply misleading.

References

1. Jon Franklin, Poisons of the Mind," *Priorities*, 9, (1997), 12

2. A.J. Dowd, Senior Vice President, American Electric Power Service Corporation, in a speech delivered before the Columbus Metropolitan Club, Columbus, Ohio, April 19, 1991

3. Associated Press, "Poll: 4 in 10 journalists have hedged on stories," *Contra Costa Times*, Section B, (May 1, 2000), 1

4. Ed Regis, *Virus Ground Zero*, (New York, Pocket Books, 1996), 235

5. Michael Fumento, *Science Under Siege*, (Quill, William Morrow, 1993), 341

6. Michael Fumento, *Science Under Siege*, 338

7. Alan K. Simpson, *Right in the Old Gazoo*, (New York, William Morrow & Company, 1997), 6, 86

8. James S. Bowman and Catherine Clarke, "American Daily Newspapers and the Environment: Attitudes of Editors, 1997 and 1992, " *International Journal of Environmental Studies*, 48, (1995), 55

9. Ben J. Wattenberg, *The Good News Is The Bad News Is Wrong*, (New York, Simon & Schuster, 1984), 112

10. Dorothy Nelkin, "Journalism and Science: The Creative Tension," in *Health Risks and the Press*, ed. Mike Moore, (Washington, D.C., The Media Institute, 1989), 59-60

11. Dean Edell and David Schrieberg, *Eat, Drink, and Be Merry*, (New York, Harper Collins, 1999), 31

12. Charles C. Mann, "Press Coverage, Leaving Out the Big Picture," *Science*, 269, (July 14, 1995), 166

13. John A. Paulos, *A Mathematician Reads the Newspapers*, (New York, Anchor Books, (1995), 29

14. Edith Efron, *The Apocalyptics: Cancer and the Big Lie*, (New York, Simon & Schuster, 1984), 473

15. Gideon Koren and Naomi Klein, "Bias Against Negative Studies in Newspaper Reports of Medical Research, *JAMA*, 266, (1991), 1824

16. Steve Wing et. al., "Mortality Among Workers at Oak Ridge National Laboratory," *JAMA*, 265, (1991), 1397

17. Seymour Jablon, Zdnek Hrubec and John D. Boice, Jr., "Cancer in Populations Living Near Nuclear Facilities," *JAMA*, 265, (1991), 1403

18. David Murray, Joel Schwartz, and S. Robert Lichter, *It Aint' Necessarily So*, (New York, Rowman & Littlefield Publishers, Inc., 2001), 150

19. Gary Taubes, "Epidemiology Faces its Limits," *Science*, 269, (July 14, 1995), 164

Chapter 26

Scientists Versus Journalists

As mentioned in "Bad News is Big News," there is an abysmal gap in communication between science and journalism and therefore, the public. As Walter Cronkite said: "Our willingness to be ignorant seems to know no bounds."[1]

"Science is literally a life-and-death news story that threads its way through every aspect of American culture – and the media leave the public mostly ill-informed about it." This is from the report, *Worlds Apart*, by Jim Hartz and Rick Chappell covering the relationship between scientists and journalists.[2] It includes results from a survey to which 762 journalists and 670 scientists responded. Here are some of the results as summarized by Tim Studt.[3]

- 91% of scientists and 77% of journalists felt that journalists lack an understanding of the nature of science and technology.
- 88% of the scientists and 56 % of the journalists felt that managers of news media are more interested in sales than in telling people what they need to know.
- 79% of the scientists and 67% of the journalists said that journalists focus on trendy issues rather than on scientific facts.
- 67% of the journalists said that they seek sensational topics that sell their product better.
- More than 50% of the scientists and journalists felt that journalists don't appreciate the need for funding basic scientific research and development.
- Journalists said that scientists' jargon and the endless qualifications by which they circumscribe their findings make communicating their work to the public an all but impossible task.

Let's look at the differences between science and journalism.

- Speed — "Science is slow, patient, precise, careful, conservative and complicated. Journalism is fast, short, hungry for headlines and drama and very imprecise at times," says Kathy Sawyer of *The Washington Post*.[4] It's a truism in news as well as in science that, as speed increases, so does the opportunity for error. In case you haven't heard the words of some anonymous author: "Doctors bury their mistakes, lawyers hang theirs, but journalists put theirs on the front page.[5]

- Language — Journalists frequently overlook or minimize the precise, qualified language that communicates the tentative nature of research findings. Scientists depend heavily on jargon.[6]

- Margin of Error — Scientists have an extraordinary advantage over journalists in that they can devise valid tests for their hypotheses. Journalists hardly ever have measurements of such precision. They are frequently thrust into exceptionally ambiguous environments in which the outcome is completely unpredictable.[7]

- Objectivity — Science, by its very nature, takes objectivity as its central premise. Journalism, on the other hand, is a largely subjective enterprise.[8] Journalists are sometimes quite open about where they stand in reporting controversies. L. Brent Bozell and Brent Baker quote Charles Alexander who said the following during a September 1989 global warming conference: "As the science editor at *Time*, I would freely admit that on this issue we have crossed the boundary from news reporting to advocacy." Bozell and Baker go on to say: "For many journalists, it's a can't-miss opportunity to demonstrate their conscience: after all, who's against saving the planet?"[9] These comments are born out by survey data reported by S. Robert Lichter and Stanley Rothman.[10] In one study, 240 randomly selected national media journalists were asked to name a reliable source on environmental problems. Sixty-nine percent mentioned environmental activist groups, while only six percent cited scientific journals such as *Science* or *Scientific American*. In the same survey, more than four out of five (81%) rejected the notion that America's environmental problems are overstated.

- Measuring Effects of Work — Scientists can accurately measure the effects of their work. Examples include vaccines which cure disease, or the Hubble telescope photographing a comet. It is different with journalists. As Hartz and Chappell note: "Journalists can seldom know anything with certitude. Accurate assessments of eventual outcomes are impossible for reporters covering the Middle East peace process, official malfeasance, the race for city council, abortion, gay rights, or the environment."[8]

Worlds Apart lists four major barriers to the effective communication of new scientific knowledge.

1. Scientists as a group are not effective or efficient in explaining their work to a lay audience. Typically, this is because scientists are not trained to communicate that knowledge to the general public. Scientists tend to be wordy, unnecessarily detailed, and overly technical. Furthermore, scientists rarely talk to journalists, and those that do are usually the ones with their own agendas, which are contrary to the thinking of the vast majority of scientists.[11] Peter Sandman points out that most journalists feel naturally more allied with their alarming sources than with their reassuring ones. He states, "This is not mostly because reporters are antiestablishment activists in disguise. It is more because reporters are interested in their careers, and a scary story is intrinsically more interesting, more important, 'better' by journalistic standards than a calming one."[12]

2. Many reporters are not familiar with the culture of science, its language and its methods. Hartz and Chappell quote Reese Cleghorn, president of the *American Journalism Review* and dean of the College of Journalism, University of Maryland: "Reporters and editors may still have the hang of politics and government and certainly the yen for covering the textures of lifestyles, but they remain largely ignorant when it comes to the sciences, for instance, where many of the new frontiers are to be found."[13]

3. Editors and producers, who decide which stories will be printed or aired, often don't feel qualified to make sound judgements about the merit of science stories. One example; of the hundreds of news managers around the nation who responded to the survey for *Worlds Apart* project, only 6% had science degrees.[14]

4. As *Worlds Apart* says: "When the once-mighty cascade of scientific and technological information finally reaches the American public, it's not much more than a trickle. Sadder still, many Americans don't know what to make of the information that gets through. They're ill-prepared to receive it."[15] Sandman states that getting

technical information into the media isn't only difficult; it's also close to useless. He uses a 1991 study as an example. He and his colleagues wrote news stories about a hypothetical perchloroethylene (PERC) spill, systematically varying three dimensions of the coverage: 1-the level of outrage (whether neighbors were angry or calm), whether the agency (New Jersey Department of Environmental Protection and Energy) was helpful or contemptuous, etc., 2-the seriousness of the spill (how much PERC was spilled, how many drinking water wells were nearby, etc.), and 3-the amount of technical information in the story. Experimental subjects were asked to read one story and answer questions about their reactions to the risk. The results: outrage had a substantial effect on risk perception; hazard had a modest effect; technical information had no effect at all.[16] Regarding this surprising outcome with technical information, Sandman has this to say: "Technical information might be expected to reassure people that the experts are on top of the situation; or it might frighten them with all those polysyllabic words and scary possibilities; best of all, it might reassure them when the hazard was low and frighten them when it was high. Instead, it simply doesn't matter or, at least, we have to find a way to make it matter. In their focus on outrage rather than hazard, journalists are at one with their audience."[17]

What to do? Carl Sagan said that scientists themselves must enter the fray, to defend both their institutions and themselves.[18] The critical questions are: How does the average scientist make himself or herself understood and appreciated, and how can the scientist's work be made relevant to the average citizen? One recommendation of the report is that all future scientists be required to take undergraduate courses in communications.[19] In addition, media training that addresses the special needs of scientists can be quite helpful. *Worlds Apart* quotes Pulitzer Prize winning author Jon Franklin: "It is time for scientists to come to terms with the fact that they're eating at a political trough and that they'd damned well better make their political case, and make it in a way that real people can understand."[20]

Here's what Elizabeth Whelan recommends in her book *Toxic Terror*:

1. Scientists must come to appreciate how irresponsible the mass media are in disseminating information, or misinformation.

2. Scientists should convince the media, by example, that scientifically sound science is not intrinsically dull.

3. Scientists, whenever possible, through personal contacts, letters to the editor, or calls to TV producers, should announce well in advance of a breaking story that they are available to answer questions on specific topics.[21]

Sandman, who consults and trains in risk communication, emphasizes that above all, when talking to the press about an environmental issue, one must be prepared to focus on outrage. He points out, "The most striking statements an environmental activist can make to the media are statements aimed at increasing, focusing and mobilizing outrage. These are the statements that are most likely to get in, and most likely to affect the audience. Conversely, the most striking statements an industry spokesperson can make to the media are statements aimed at reducing outrage: acknowledgment of problems, apologies for misbehaviors, offers to share control, explanations of what the source is doing and what the audience can do to mitigate the risk, demonstrations of accountability in lieu of trust, etc. Sources who are convinced it is trivial, on the other hand, usually make the mistake of believing the key task is to explain the data."[22]

The evidence points to both the scientist and the journalist as the cause of misinformation on scientific (specifically environmental) issues. Who is more at fault, and what should be done?

References

1. Walter Cronkite, quoted in Jim Hartz and Rick Chappell, *Worlds Apart: How the Distance Between Science and Journalism Threatens America's Future*, (Nashville, Tennessee, First Amendment Center, 1997), 25

2. Jim Hartz and Rick Chappell, *Worlds Apart: How the Distance Between Science and Journalism Threatens America's Future*, viii

3. Tim Studt, "Science and Journalism Can Work Together," *R&D Magazine*, 13 (June 1998), 40

4. Jim Hartz and Rick Chappell, *Worlds Apart: How the Distance Between Science and Journalism Threatens America's Future*, 14

5. Jim Hartz and Rick Chappell, *Worlds Apart: How the Distance Between Science and Journalism Threatens America's Future*, 47

6. Jim Hartz and Rick Chappell, *Worlds Apart: How the Distance Between Science and Journalism Threatens America's Future*, 15

7. Jim Hartz and Rick Chappell, *Worlds Apart: How the Distance Between Science and Journalism Threatens America's Future*, 16

8. Jim Hartz and Rick Chappell, *Worlds Apart: How the Distance Between Science and Journalism Threatens America's Future*, 17

9. *And That's The Way It Is(n't)*, eds. L. Brent Bozell III and Brent H. Baker, (Alexandria, Virginia, Media Research Center, 1990), 109

10. S. Robert Lichter and Stanley Rothman, *Environmental Cancer - A Political Disease*, (New Haven, Connecticut, Yale University Press, 1999), 169

11. Jim Hartz and Rick Chappell, *Worlds Apart: How the Distance Between Science and Journalism Threatens America's Future*, 21

12. Peter M. Sandman, "Mass Media and Environmental Risk: Seven Principles," in *What Risk?*, ed., Roger Bate, (Oxford, Butterworth Heineman, 1997), 282

13. Jim Hartz and Rick Chappell, *Worlds Apart: How the Distance Between Science and Journalism Threatens America's Future*, 22

14. Jim Hartz and Rick Chappell, *Worlds Apart: How the Distance Between Science and Journalism Threatens America's Future*, 58

15. Jim Hartz and Rick Chappell, *Worlds Apart: How the Distance Between Science and Journalism Threatens America's Future*, 24

16. Branden B. Johnson, Peter M. Sandman, and Paul Miller, "Testing the Role of Technical Information in Public Risk Perception," *RISK-Issues in Health & Safety*, 341, (Fall 1992), 3

17. Peter M. Sandman, "Mass Media and Environment Risk: Seven Principles," 277

18. Jim Hartz and Rick Chappell, *Worlds Apart: How the Distance Between Science and Journalism Threatens America's Future*, 91

19. Jim Hartz and Rick Chappell, *Worlds Apart: How the Distance Between Science and Journalism Threatens America's Future*, 94

20. Jim Hartz and Rick Chappell, *Worlds Apart: How the Distance Between Science and Journalism Threatens America's Future*, 98

21. Elizabeth M. Whelan, *Toxic Terror*, (Ottawa, Illinois, Jameson Books, 1985), 293

22. Peter M. Sandman, "Mass Media and Environment Risk: Seven Principles," 283

Chapter 27

Environmental Education — Breeding Brain-washed Activists?

Have you ever heard of Chief Seattle? He was the leader of the Puget Sound Indian tribe and is credited with delivering a speech in 1855 that resonated with environmental relevance, a Gettysburg-like oration for the environmentalist movement. It has been quoted in Al Gore's book *Earth in the Balance*, the autobiography of U.S. Supreme Court Justice William Douglas, in countless articles, has been broadcast in at least six foreign countries, and a children's book about the speech sold more than 250,000 copies and was listed as number 5 on the *New York Times* best-sellers list for nonfiction in 1992. There is even a popular Chinese version of the book.

All this for something that is an utter lie.

Chief Seattle never penned these words. They came from Ted Perry, a university professor hired to write a TV documentary about pollution in 1972. He decided to create a fictional version of Seattle's response to territorial officials' offer to buy tribal land.[1] Here's an excerpt of what Seattle (Professor Perry) said.

"Every part of this earth is sacred to my people. Every shining pine needle, every sandy shore, every mist in the dark woods, every meadow, every humming insect...The earth is our mother...What befalls the earth befalls all the sons and daughters of the earth."

This is just an example of how adults, and most importantly to this chapter, children, are being brainwashed into becoming ignorant activists.

"As our nation continues its all-consuming pursuit of protecting the environment, 'regardless of the cost,' we are overlooking the greatest cost of all: the toll on our children." These are words from Jo Kwong who conducted an extensive review on "environmental education." She discovered a number of unsettling trends and strategies. She reports:

1. Children are being scared into becoming environmental activists.

2. Material about the environment aimed at children contains widespread misinformation.

3. Children are being taught **what to think**, not **how to think**.

4. Children are taught that human beings are evil.

5. Children feel helpless and pessimistic about their future on earth.

6. Environmental education is being used to undermine the simple joys of childhood.[2]

Charles Sykes reports: "A review by the Arizona Institute for Public Policy Research of 82 textbooks, 170 environmental books for children and 84 examples of curriculum materials provided to schools by environmental groups (and adopted uncritically for classroom instruction) found 'that unbiased materials present only one side of the issue, pick only worst case examples, or simply omit information that challenges an apocalyptic outlook.'"[3]

The schools' teachings are having a powerful effect. Julian Simon notes: "The consensus view of an informal *Fortune* survey of high schoolers on this issue was: If we continue at the pace we're going at now, the environment is going to be destroyed completely. A 1992 poll found that 47% of a sample of 6-17 year olds said that 'Environment' is among the biggest problems in our country these days; 12% mentioned 'Economy' as a distant runner-up. Compare this to what their parents thought: 13% 'Environment' versus 56% 'Economy.'"[4]

Here are some other examples. Simon notes the following: "A kids page in the Sunday paper purveys such bits of 'obvious wisdom' as 'It takes more than 500,000 trees to make the newspapers that Americans read on Sunday...we're running out of places to put it...there aren't very many places to put [landfills].' The children are not told that trees are grown, and forests created, in order to make newspaper."[5] In reporting on environmental 'science' in the classroom

Michael Sanera and Jane Shaw report that "Children are taught that acid rain caused by emissions from power plants and automobiles destroys lakes and forests. They are told to mix vinegar with water and to pour it on plants to see the plants die. They do not learn that this mixture does not resemble 'acid rain,' or that a $500 million government study showed that acid rain is causing harm in only a few places."[6] More than 70 characters in Marvel comic books developed severe physical and emotional handicaps as a consequence of exposure to radiation. "The message inherent in the experience of these characters is communicated effectively to young persons and for that matter to many others who are not so young," says William Hendee.[7] A book entitled *Nuclear Power-Promise or Peril*, by Michael J. Daley is touted by the publisher as an accurate and evenhanded treatment of nuclear power but is rife with inaccuracies and antinuclear messages. Carl E. Walter observes: "Although technical errors load an error-ridden database into readers minds, the true disservice to readers lies in the sometimes subliminal and often explicit unsubstantiated messages interleaved throughout the book that nuclear power is a peril – not a promise. Purportedly unbiased, actually it is not. In fact, the book is dedicated to two individuals who are associated with antinuclear groups, and Daley himself belongs to one of the groups. What really bothers me is that *The Science Teacher*, a reputable U.S. magazine directed at high school teachers nationwide, published a glowing review in support of the book. Our high school students deserve accurate technical information and clear and objective discussion of social positions on technology, not the misinformation presented by the book or its review."[8]

Bev Graves reports that her son did not learn at school that most industries have to treat the water before it is discharged; even though at home we could pour the same chemicals down the drain. "To them, muddy water is polluted, anything pouring out of a smoke stack, even steam, is polluting the air."[9]

Before we discuss what to do about this, Jennifer Sahn observes in the introduction to David Sobel's book *Beyond Ecophobia*: "In our desire to prepare the next generation of adults to deal with the legacy of our ecological assaults, there is a tendency to inform children of the problems concerning the human-nature relationship while failing to share with them its beautiful possibilities. In rushing to teach them about global issues and responsible activism, we neglect the fact that young children have a fascination with the immediate, and an undying curiosity that requires direct sensory experience rather than conceptual generalization.[10] *Beyond Ecophobia* presents environmental education strategies for teachers and parents of young people that cater to a child's natural affinities. "The key is in allowing for a close relationship to develop between children and the nature near home before laying the weight of the world's plight on their shoulders."

Make yourself aware of what your children (nieces/nephews/grandchildren, etc.) are learning about the environment in school. Do not take it for granted that they are getting both sides of the story. We want our children to develop critical thinking skills, but to do so they have to hear both sides of the story.

One organization that is working on the problem is PERC (The Political Economy Research Center) in Bozeman, Montana. It has developed programs to help middle and high school students think about the environment. It also publishes a newsletter for teachers and high school students called *Environmental Examiner*, and sponsors teacher workshops around the country.

If you are looking for books, try *Facts, Not Fear*, by Michael Sanera and Jane Shaw. This is a good guidebook to help parents counter the irresponsible claims of environmental extremists — and to give their children a more balanced view of the many environmental issues they encounter. In simple, nontechnical language, the authors explain the myths and facts concerning many major environmental topics and show you how to set the record straight for the kids. Another book is *A Blueprint for Environmental Education*, by Jane Shaw, which discusses the current state of environmental education.

Sanera and Shaw sum it up quite well: "Environmental education could be a valuable part of science instruction. Instead, it often merely repeats the nostrums of the environmental movement, and molds children into smug crusaders whose foundation of knowledge is shaky at best.[6]

There is nothing wrong with teaching students about environmental issues; in fact, it is very important. However, shouldn't they be taught the true scientific and economic complexity of these issues?

When biased and misleading information about environmental issues such as global warming is used to recruit our children as shock troops in a crusade to support a particular political agenda, aren't we doing them a great disservice?

References

1. Mary Murray, "The Little Green Lie," *Reader's Digest*, (July 1993), 100

2. Jo Kwong, "EcoKids: New Automatons on the Block," *The Freeman*, 45, (March 1995), 155

3. Charles J. Sykes, *Dumbing Down Our Kids*, (New York, St. Martin's Press, 1995), 138

4. Julian L. Simon, *The Ultimate Resource 2*, (Princeton, New Jersey, Princeton University Press, 1996), 214

5. Julian L. Simon, *The Ultimate Resource 2*, 275

6. Michael Sanera and Jane S. Shaw, "Environmental 'Science' in the Classroom," *Consumers Research*, 80, (April 1997), 15

7. William R. Hendee, "Public Perceptions of Radiation Risks," in *Radiation and Public Perception: Benefits and Risks*, eds., Jack P. Young and Rosalyn S. Yalow, (Washington, D.C., American Chemical Society, 1995), 21

8. Carl E. Walter, "Nuclear misinformation," *Nuclear News*, 42, (January 1999), 34

9. Bev Graves, "Whose Fault is it that Your Neighbor Knows Nothing About Finishing?," *Products Finishing*, 61, (March 1997), 6

10. David Sobel, *Beyond Ecophobia*, (Great Barrington, Massachusetts, The Orion Society, 1996), vi

Chapter 28

Statistics — Speaking with Forked Tongues

Joel Best, in his book, *Damned Lies and Statistics*, wrote the perfect opening to this chapter. "There are cultures in which people believe that some objects have magical powers; anthropologists call these objects fetishes. In our society, statistics are a sort of fetish. We tend to regard them as though they are magical, as though they are more than mere numbers. We treat them as powerful representations of the truth; we act as though they distill the complexity and confusion of reality into simple facts. We use statistics to convert complicated social problems into more easily understood estimates, percentages, and rates. Statistics direct our concern; they show us what we ought to worry about and how much we ought to worry. In a sense, the social problem becomes the statistics as true and incontrovertible, they achieve a kind of fetish-like, magical control over how we view social problems. We think of statistics as facts we discover, not as numbers we create."[1]

Whenever we see or hear numbers within reports, there is almost an automatic response to them as truth. They shape our thinking about issues, and you can often hear people quoting numbers in discussion. How many times have you heard "the numbers don't lie" in an argument? Well, the fact is, activists in all forums (social, environmental, etc.) use statistics to support their particular points of view, when all too often, **these numbers are lying**. As Rex Stout says: "There are two types of statistics, the kind you look up, and the kind you make up."[2]

What follows are several examples of statistics (numbers) that are misreported, misrepresented, and outright false. As you will see throughout, the media are not immune to misreporting statistics and commonly repeat the figures given by sources without checking the facts behind the numbers. As Joel Best says: "Reporters want to report facts, activists' numbers look like facts, and it may be difficult, even impossible to find other numbers, so the media tend to report the activists' figures. And once a number appears in one news report, that report is a potential source for everyone who becomes interested in the social problem; officials, experts, activists, and other reporters routinely repeat figures that appear in press reports. The number takes on a life of its own, people repeat bad statistics."[3]

Let's start with a fun one. Sometimes, it's not that two bits of data contradict one another; it's that the same bit of data can be read (or presented) in at least two ways. During the Cold War, a two-car race (one Soviet, one American) took place and we'll compare coverage in the press on both sides. An American newspaper headline read "American car beats out Soviet competitor." The Russian newspaper headline read "Soviet car finishes second; American car is next-to-last." So, what do these both mean? Well, the American's won the race, but the reader is certainly left with different impressions.[4] Obviously, the Soviet press did not want to admit defeat, so in changing the expression of the same information, made it sound much different. Read on, and see how numbers are doctored in their expression.

A common form of mutant statistic involves the transformation of a number's meaning. Usually, this involves someone who tries to repeat a number, but confuses the facts attached to the figure. Joel Best uses the example of anorexia nervosa in young women. "Activists seeking to draw attention to the problem estimated that some 150,000 American women suffer from anorexia. At some point, feminists began reporting that each year 150,000 women died from anorexia. This was a considerable exaggeration; about 70 deaths per year are attributed to anorexia. This simple transformation, turning an estimate for the total number of anorexic women into the annual number of fatalities — produced a dramatic, memorable statistic. Advocates repeated the erroneous figure in influential books, in newspaper columns, on talk shows, and so on.[5] So, if you heard that 150,000 women died every year from anorexia, you would believe it to be a major problem in the United States, right? If you heard it was only 70, then perhaps you would not be as concerned? The activists know this, and may change the expression to make sure you are concerned, and therefore support them in their activities against anorexia.

John Paulos illustrates a good point: "If the number at issue is a sum or product, or is otherwise mathematically dependent on several other numbers, only one of them need to be imprecise for this imprecision to infect the given number. The joke is about the museum guard who told visitors that the dinosaur on exhibit was 90,000,006 years old. Upon questioning, the guard explained that he was told the dinosaur was 90,000,000 years old when he was hired, six years before."[6]

Another example involves a dissertation for a research project leading to a Ph.D. that began with this statement: "Every year since 1950, the number of American children gunned down has doubled." Joel Best thought that the student had made an error in copying the figure from the source, but when he checked the journal's 1995 volume he found the exact same sentence.

So what's so bad about the "grabber" statement? Assume that one child was gunned down in 1950. If the number doubled every year, as the statement says, by the time we reached the 1980s, over 2 billion children per year in the United States were being killed by guns. Best tracked down the original source of the statistic, the Children's Defense Fund (CDF). The CDF yearbook of 1994 states: "The number of children killed each year by guns has doubled since 1950." Note that CDF claimed there were twice as many deaths in 1994 as in 1950, yet the article the graduate student referenced had *reworded* the claim and created a very different meaning. Neither the graduate student, the author of the original journal article, nor the editor of the journal which published the original paper examined the statistic and realized it had to be incorrect.[7] All too often, bad statistics endure because no one questions them and points out their flaws.

Be cautious when you hear some disease has suddenly increased in numbers. Statistics on mortality data produced by the National Center for Health Statistics (NCHS) have undergone a number of significant revisions. Rodger Doyle reports: "Under the protocols of the World Health Organizations's International Classification of Diseases, 10th Revision, which went into effect in the U.S. with the 1999 data, the NCHS has substantially changed the data for many causes of death. A notable one is Alzheimer's, which will jump by at least 55 percent above the level reported for 1998. This increase does not reflect a sudden surge in mortality but a change in classification."[8] Can you see how easy it would be to misinterpret the 55 percent raise in mortality due to Alzheimer's disease here?

Joel Best notes, "There is deliberate manipulation, conscious attempts to turn statistical information to particular uses. Data can be presented in ways that convey different impressions, and it is not uncommon for advocates to choose selectively which numbers they report, and to pick with care the words they use to describe the figures. That is, some numbers are selected because they promise to persuade, to support the advocates positions. This need not be dishonest; advocates making a case can make it clear that they've chosen to interpret statistics in particular ways. But very often the questionable interpretive work remains hidden, and we have every reason to be suspicious of both the numbers and the advocates' honesty when mutations are concealed from the audience."[9] World Health Organization director Christopher Murray reports, "Cancer fighters tell you that their crisis is deepening, and more research money is urgently needed. Those doing battle with malaria make similar pronouncements, as do those working on TB (tuberculosis). If all the claims are added, you wind up with a theoretical death toll that 'exceeds' the number of humans who die annually by two-to-threefold."[10]

Extrapolation is the process of prediction by projecting past experience or known data. This is a technique used by activists, often to "raise awareness." However, sometimes they extrapolate data to the point of ridiculousness.

The icon of American beauty, Miss America is becoming thinner and thinner report researchers at Johns Hopkins University. Body Mass Index (BMI), the in vogue technique for measuring body thinness (or obesity) dropped from 22 for Miss America in 1920 to 17 for Miss America in 1990. At this rate, according to *Time*, the BMI of Miss America in 320 years would be zero.[12]

Even Mark Twain blasted scientists about 130 years ago, summing up the nonsense of extrapolation in *Life on the Mississippi*: "Now if I wanted to be one of those ponderous scientific people, and 'let on' to prove what had occurred in the remote past by what had occurred in a given time in the recent past, or what will occur in the far future by what has occurred in last year, what an opportunity is here! In the space of one hundred seventy six years the Lower Mississippi has shortened itself two hundred forty five miles. That is an average of a trifle over one mile and a third per year. Therefore, any calm person, who is not blind or idiotic, can see that in the Old Oolitic Silurian Period, just a million years ago next November, the Lower Mississippi River was upward of one million three hundred thousand miles long, and stuck out over the Gulf of Mexico like a fishing rod. And by the same token any person can see that seven hundred and forty two years from now, the Lower Mississippi will only be a mile and three-quarters long. There is something fascinating about science. One gets such wholesale returns of conjecture out of such a trifling investment of fact."[13]

One final tool that science and activists use to gain attention is the "relative risk" method. Here's an example.

Which of these two headlines is likely to get more attention?

1. YEARLY STOOL TEST REDUCES COLON CANCER DEATHS BY 33 PERCENT
   -or-
2. YEARLY STOOL TEST REDUCES YOUR CHANCE OF COLON CANCER DEATH BY LESS THAN 1 PERCENT

Both are accurate statements from a very large study (46,951 participants) but one speaks to *relative risk reduction* while the other covers *individual risk reduction*. In the group that received annual screening for blood in the stool, 2.6 percent died of colon cancer, while 3.4 percent of those in the group that did not receive annual screening died of colon cancer. The relative risk reduction was 33 percent. However, the individual risk reduction (i.e. the difference between 2.6 and 3.4 percent) is 0.8 percent. Therefore, the chance that annual screening for blood in the stool will prevent **you** from dying of colon cancer is less than one percent. Clearly, the headline that suggests a 33 percent reduction will get the attention.[14]

Donald Murphy states, "The medical profession and the media advertise *relative risk reduction* and not individual risk reduction, and no matter how sophisticated the research project and statistics may be, interpretation of the data can vary."[14]

A good way to sum up the problem with the use of statistics is to borrow a phrase from the myriad of infomercials on late night TV: "Individual results may vary." When activists and scientists use statistics as "proof" of their stances on issues, we all must be wary of how their numbers are being presented. All too often, these numbers are being skewed to bring issues to the forefront, and take full advantage of the American idea that "the numbers never lie."

References

1. Joel Best, *Damned Lies and Statistics*, (Berkeley, California, University of California Press, 2001), 160

2. Rex Stout quoted in Steven J. Milloy, *Junk Science Judo*, (Washington, D.C., Cato Institute, 2001), 115

3. Joel Best, *Damned Lies and Statistics*, 35

4. David Murray, Joel Schwartz and S. Robert Lichter, *It Ain't Necessarily So*, (New York, Rowan & Littlefield Publishers, 2001), 86

5. Joel Best, *Damned Lies and Statistics*, 63

6. John A. Paulos, *A Mathematician Reads the Newspaper*, (New York, Anchor Books, 1995), 172

7. Joel Best, *Damned Lies and Statistics*, 2

8. Rodger Doyle, "Rewriting History," *Scientific American*, 284, (May 2001), 26

9. Joel Best, *Damned Lies and Statistics*, 94

10. Christopher Murray quoted in Rian Malan, "Megadeath and Megahype," *San Francisco Chronicle*, (January 6, 2002), D1

11. John A. Paulos, *A Mathematician Reads the Newspaper*, 15

12. "Missing America," *Time Magazine*, 155, (April 3, 2000), 22

13. Mark Twain, *Life on the Mississippi*, (New York, Harper & Row, 1874), 142

14. Donald J. Murphy, *Honest Medicine*, (New York, The Atlantic Monthly Press, 1995), 26

Chapter 29

Environmentalism and Cultural Differences —
The "Envirocrats"

In 1992, the United Nations Conference on Environment and Development was held in Rio de Janeiro. Mark Dowie reported: "No one who attended the nongovernmental organizations' (NGO) preparatory meetings in New York would have been surprised by the behavior of American environmentalists in Rio. There and in Rio, third-world delegates found them to be imperious and insensitive." 'We don't want to be lectured as to what we should do, unless it is done in a cooperative and democratic way,' said delegate Main Shankar. 'I am not about to go to my people and tell them they must face more deprivation because some lady in Maine is fretting over the cutting of a tree or because some chap in San Francisco wants to drive his Volvo in better conscience. We can sit down and talk when we realize that one job in Cincinnati is not one bit more important than one job in New Delhi.'[1]

What means one thing in a first world country can mean something quite different in developing countries. For instance, when the Pepsi slogan, "Come alive with the Pepsi generation" was translated into Chinese, it was understood as "Pepsi brings your ancestors back from the grave." Culturally-rooted beliefs that influence behavior patterns in developing countries can interfere with the application of environmental and health remedies that were developed in the industrialized world.[2]

John Harte provides this example. "At a scientific meeting in Beijing in 1983, I was pleased to learn that the Chinese were beginning to study acid rain. I was less pleased to recognize the tremendous gulf between what we in the West mean. In China the term 'pollution standard' means a prediction, not an enforceable limit. They calculate what pollution levels are likely to be under plausible assumptions about fuel consumption and meager government spending on pollution control. They call the result of the calculation a 'standard.' If it is exceeded it is not the factories that get the blame; it is the person who worked out the estimate."[3] What's the point of this example? What we believe is not always what other cultures see as the same truth.

Sometimes developing countries get caught in the middle and because of political pressure, end up in situations worse than before the changes were made. As Robert Desowitz explains, "Health professionals working in the tropical regions have largely ignored modification of behavior as a means of disease control. Nor have they taken into account the behavior and beliefs of the target populations when designing health campaigns. The notion persists among health authorities that high-technology panaceas can, by themselves, be effective. Many are surprised when their drugs, vaccines, and sanitation projects are rejected or allowed to fall into disuse."[2]

The following example from Desowitz involving toilets in Somalia shows the problems that can arise when countries in the first world try to help countries in transition in areas of health and environment. "Health advisors from a Western nation were appalled by the toilet habits of the Somalis. The entire country seemed to be covered with indiscriminately scattered human feces. Hardly a toilet, flush or any other kind, was to be found in this impoverished nation. Fecally transmitted parasitic, bacterial, and viral diseases were rife. So with all the best intentions, these experts decided to use their government's aid funds for a pilot project that would provide simple water-seal toilets to a selected village. In due course, several hundred of the cast concrete devices were placed over soak-away pits that had been laboriously dug to the prescribed dimensions. The advisers then returned to their office in the capital, satisfied that they had propelled these people onto the road to modern sanitation." A year later when the experts returned, they found the toilets to be horrible messes. Each one was stuffed with a pile of stones and made useless. When the advisers asked why anyone would dump stones into a toilet, their respondent was surprised. The elder noted that Somalis distract themselves while defecating by clicking two stones together and when finished they dropped the stones into the most convenient receptacle — the water toilet seat.[2]

Lorraine Mooney and Roger Bate caution against exporting inappropriate attitudes from developed to less-developed countries. They present case studies of malaria in South Africa and Peru that show the fatal consequences of allowing western preoccupations with trivial risks (such as the cancer effects of pesticide residues in foods and chlorine compounds in water) to influence health policy in the third world.[4] I would suggest reading (or re-reading) the chapter on DDT to see the full scope of the fatal consequences Mooney and Bate are discussing.

Stuart Nagel, in his recent book, provides some examples from the Philippines. "The first example involves informing farmers as to how they can double their crops through better seeds, pesticides, herbicides, fertilizer, and machinery, but not providing for any increased storage facilities to put the doubled crop. The result was that much of the increased productivity rotted in the fields. The second example involved informing farmers how they could arrange for as many as four crops per year, instead of one crop per year, through special seeds that have a three month season. The crops thus go from being put into the ground to being ready to harvest every three months. The farmers, however, were not informed as to how one person could plow, weed, and harvest four times a year, and still be able to attend fiestas."[5]

Haile Asmerom discusses the United Nations Environmental Program (UNEP) meant to serve as a catalyst and coordinator for various global programs. He says, "The fact that it is located far away from the regions where its activities were to be carried out means that it has no control over what is going on in the designated areas. For this very reason alone, it has been described as a toothless tiger trying to wield authority from a distance."[6]

Tim Flannery reports that conservation programs in countries such as Papau, New Guinea are fraught with difficulty because Western notions of conservation often appear to be completely nonsensical to the local people. "Many villagers believe that the animals of the forest have always been there and that they will always remain. When faced with clear evidence of a decline in abundance, or even extinction, they will point to a place over the mountain saying 'There' still plenty there.' Little do they realize there is always a village 'over there,' inhabited by people, who when asked the same question, point back in their own direction."[7]

Communication across linguistic barriers can also present a prob-lem. For instance, Inuktitut, the preferred language of most Inuit living in the Eastern and Central Arctic has no equivalent for many of the scientific concepts and terms typically used in discussing chemical contaminants. Douglas Powell and William Leiss state, "Inasmuch as the notion of industrial contaminants and of their detection by scien-tific means falls outside the sphere of traditional experiences, indig-enous populations have been inclined to interpret contaminant in-formation in the light of past experiences with outsiders. Because con-tact with southern visitors and the transition from living on the land to settlement life brought about profound changes in the living con-ditions of northern aborigines, they have grown wary about external interventions. As a result, contaminant information and advice pro-vided by scientists and other outside experts tends to be received with various degrees of skepticism, suspicion, and mistrust."[8]

Michael Parfit, in an article in *National Geographic* describes the Inuit lifestyle in detail typical of that magazine. Without even getting into the complexities of environmental issues, he asks these funda-mental questions. "How do you regulate hunting and fishing to re-flect the Inuit need for food, the profound Inuit attitude towards ani-mals, and the Inuit skill with modern weapons? And how do you cre-ate a viable cash economy in a society just one generation away from a subsistence way of life?"[9]

I am reminded as I write this of a roundtable discussion in the 1980s at Marist College regarding why minority groups were not being more involved in a project to conserve "green space" on the Hudson River. Although I cannot quote any specific data or person, I do remember the gist of one comment from a prominent New York City minister. He believed that it wasn't that minorities did not care about the environ-ment, but that they were more concerned with day-to-day survival than about someone's desire to ride their bike next to the Hudson River.

One of the most fascinating parts of this rock hurtling through the void of space is culture. I believe that differing ideas of how to live life is just as important as the air we breathe. Do we not all in some way try to emulate other cultures in order to enjoy or better our lives? As seen in the examples, the western desire to "fix" every-thing often falls on deaf ears, or comes up against unforeseen obstacles. Our ethnocentric philosophy can have negative results on other cultures, sometimes so extreme as to cause death. At the very least, indigenous peoples who are trying to simply survive do not understand the desire of some folks to preserve a tree or an animal. That tree may provide shelter or be used in other fashions, while that animal is dinner for a starving family. I used the word "envirocrats" in the title of this chapter for a reason. Is this environmentally aristocratic desire to have their agendas followed more important than the "needs" of those they are affecting?

References

1. Mark Dowie, *Losing Ground*, (Cambridge, Massachusetts, The MIT Press, 1997), 167

2. Robert S. Desowitz, *New Guinea Tapeworms and Jewish Grandmothers: Tales of Parasites and People*, (New York, W.W. Norton & Co., 1987), 187

3. John Harte, *The Green Fuse*, (Berkeley, University of California Press, 1993), 137

4. *Environmental Health: Third World Problems – First World Preoccupations*, eds., Lorraine Mooney and Roger Bate, (Oxford, Butterworth Heinemann, 1999), 1 and 17

5. Stuart S. Nagel, "Environmental Policy and Super-Optimum Solutions," in *Environmental Policy and Developing Nations*, Stuart S. Nagel, (Jefferson, North Carolina, McFarland and Company, Inc., 2002), 11

6. Haile K. Asmerom, "Bureaucracy and Environmental Policy in the Sahel Region of Africa: Strategies for Arresting the March of Desertification," in *Environmental Policy and Developing Nations*, ed., Stuart S. Nagel, (Jefferson, North Carolina, McFarland and Company, Inc., 2002), 58

7. Tim F. Flannery, *Throwim Way Leg: Tree Kangaroos, Possums, and Penis Gourds - On the Track of Unknown Mammals in Wildest New Guinea.*, (Boston, Atlantic Monthly Press, 1998), 200

8. Douglas Powell and William Leiss, *Mad Cows and Mother's Milk*, (Montreal, McGill-Queen's University Press, 1997), 204

9. Michael Parfit, "A Dream Called Nunavut," *National Geographic*, 192, (September 1997), 68

Chapter 30

Environmental Hysteria — Funny Stories, Serious Morals

Imagine this scene. You are watching TV, and the screen goes black. For a moment, there is nothing, until ominous music starts to play and slowly the screen fills in with the image of a common backyard swimming pool somewhere in America. There are no children playing, no inflated toys, and the water is dead calm. A woman's voice, full of concern speaks in a concerned voice. "Do you realize there is enough water here to drown 100,000 people?" The screen then fades to black as the music lulls, and you see the ad was sponsored by The Ad Council and CAPOW (Citizens Against Pool OWners).

Of course, this is a farcical ad, based on an idea from Elizabeth Whelan in her book *Toxic Terror*. However, a hysteria has taken over concerning our environment. Activists have drummed into our heads for so long that anything man-made (especially chemicals) is dangerous or that we as a species are destroying everything around us, that we cannot think rationally. I am not accusing everyone of being irrational, but here are some excellent examples of how activism has thwarted the American consciousness, on both the private and public levels.

Washington lobbyist Peter Sparber wanted to prove how easy it is to drum up an environmental scare. According to the *Omaha World Herald*, he put together a mailing list of people on record favoring a ban on pesticides and sent them a letter from a fictitious organization warning them about the need to stop the production of dihydrogen oxide. He claimed in the letter that dihydrogen oxide was responsible for 4,100 deaths in a recent year and awaited a response. Letters poured in scolding the "evil producers" of this chemical. Unfortunately, each letter proved that the recipients were scientific illiterates, because the horrible chemical they supported banning was, water. Sparber "proved his point and showed how easy it is to turn scientific illiteracy into environmental hysteria," reports *Citizen Outlook.*[1]

Alston Chase, a nationally syndicated columnist relates this story. "Call it fear of spraying. In one study, researchers spewed distilled water from planes over residential neighborhoods without telling anyone what the spray contained. The intent was to gauge public phobia of chemicals. And sure enough, the experimenters were soon deluged with complaints from frightened folks who claimed the spray was causing cows to abort, dogs to shed, and children to get sick."[2]

Ronald Gots reported in February 1997 of an incident at Washington's Reagan National Airport. "When someone reported smelling a 'noxious gas' in a terminal, evacuation was ordered. Hundreds of people fell ill. A hazardous-materials crew in protective suits combed the building and found the culprit — rotting bananas in a trash can."[3]

A 1996 article in *Reason* described how a woman hung her mail on a clothesline for weeks before reading it, to allow the "toxins" in the ink to dissipate.[4]

Stephen Barrett and Ronald Gots reported the following in 1985. "A Bell South facility in Orange County, California had a sudden outbreak of fainting episodes. The building was evacuated, hazardous material and fire department teams combed the building seeking a cause, and affected workers were taken to local hospitals for treatment. Examinations of both the building and the workers did not reveal any noxious chemicals or measurable physical damage to the workers. Ultimately, it was determined that a disgruntled worker had started a rumor about a dangerous chemical loose in the building."[5]

All these examples concerning private citizens, show how environmental and social activism can affect the rationality of everyday people. Just the thought of exposure to a chemical can cause sickness or hysteria. Logic was thrown out the window in every case.

Here's a case that proves that some environmental activists have no real knowledge about the science behind their claims.

Several environmental activists attended a meeting of toxicologists in Cambridge, Massachusetts in which the toxicologists were talking about the LD_{50} of some chemicals. LD_{50} is a term used to express the amount of a toxin that will kill 50 percent of a given species at a specific dose. For example, the LD_{50} of azobenzene is 1,000mg/kg for rats. So, at the dose of 1,000mg/kg, 50% of the rats in a study of azobenzene died. At the meeting, after hearing about LD_{50} for this chemical and LD_{50} for that chemical, one of the activists chimed in "Well if the LD_{50} is such a problem, why not get rid of that chemical?"[6] The activist showed a total lack of knowledge, yet still proposed a ban.

Here's one that is just funny.

People for the Ethical Treatment of Animals (PETA) have called on Fishkill, New York to change its name to "Fishsave." A little history lesson here, folks at PETA. Fishkill is a 300 year old town founded by Dutch settlers. In Dutch, the word "kill" means "creek."[7] I haven't heard yet if PETA is trying to get the Catskills renamed, but won't be surprised when I do.

However, PETA and other animal activists have pressured our government so much that rules and regulations concerning endangered species have permeated our existence at almost every level. Peter Huber notes that the Endangered Species Act pays no respect at all to the notion that public interests must somehow be kept separate from private ones, and offers the following example. "If an endangered tapeworm happened to find refuge in your intestine, it would be a federal crime for you to consume the medicine that rendered your guts uninhabitable to your guest. The same goes for endangered cockroaches under your floorboards, or an endangered strain of typhoid in your water well. There is no private left, not body, not floorboard, land, home, or farm, not once an officially endangered species has designated it as its habitat."[8]

As mentioned, the pressures put on our governing bodies by activists have brought hysteria to our body of laws in the United States. Here are some examples of environmental regulations that make no sense at all.

The first is from *Citizen Outlook*. "Taking the floor of the U.S. Senate each day for more than a week, Orrin Hatch, the Senator from

Utah took out his 'Top 10 List of Silly Regulations,' and, doing his best impersonation of David Letterman, shared with his colleagues one account after another of a federal bureaucracy gone awry. He told them how Uncle Sam requires buildings to be inspected for asbestos, even if they were built after the asbestos ban took effect and therefore contain no asbestos. He told them how one company was prosecuted for 'conspiring to knowingly transport hazardous waste' after the company had discharged waste water that contained 0.0003 percent of methylene chloride — even though decaffeinated coffee has a higher percentage. He also told them how the Coast Guard attempted to fine the owner of a van \$5,000 for 'polluting the waters of the United States' after the van had been in an accident, leaked 2 gallons of gasoline, and the local fire department flushed it down a nearby drain. The Senator's point was that government regulations, although perhaps well intentioned, have simply passed the point of sensibility. Many of the regulations have become way too picayune, and are slowly choking the lifeblood out of the small businesses that form the backbone of our nation's economy."[9]

Dixy Lee Ray's favorite example of nonsensical regulations concerns the EPA and the city of Anchorage, Alaska. Proof positive that "too often the rules and regulations which are made to apply uniformly throughout the country do not make sense when applied to a specific region." She states: "under the 1987 amendment to the Clean Water Act, city sewage plants must remove 30% of the organic material from the municipal sewage. Now with Anchorage, the problem is this: Their sewage was heavily diluted with rainwater, to the point that not only was there almost no detectable organic material in there, but the amount was so small that physically, chemically it was impossible to comply with the regulation from the EPA. So naturally, they asked for a variance. The word came back, no, the law is the law — you will take 30 percent of the organics out of the sewage. So the city officials thought about this a bit, and found a solution. They made a contract with three different fish processing plants in the city of Anchorage and required the fish processors to put all their fish guts and waste into the city sewage. Then they had enough organic materials so they could remove 30 percent of it, and the EPA was very happy."[10] Imagine, having to further taint the sewage, just to comply with a regulation.

Here's another item from Alaska from a press release posted by the Alaska State Library. "The EPA has agreed with Governor Tony Knowles' request to allow Alaska to continue to use state, not federal water quality standards for arsenic. Knowles petitioned the federal government last year to allow Alaska to use the state's original arsenic water quality standard. Alaska's standard was overridden when the EPA imposed the National Toxics Rule on the state, reducing the arsenic standard *well below naturally existing conditions.* In his petition, Knowles noted that the federal standard for a wastewater discharge was 277 times more restrictive than the standard for drinking water. Under the federal rule, it would have been okay to drink a glass of water from an Alaskan stream, but you couldn't pour any of that water back because of the level of naturally occurring arsenic."[11]

One last example from Citizen Outlook. "Not too long ago, the little town of Washington, Georgia, had a not-so-little problem with the EPA. It seems the agency was threatening to fine the town $50,000 per day because its waste water had not passed toxicity tests. According to The Washington Times, it wasn't any particular toxic pollutant the EPA was worried about, but rather, the simple fact that laboratory-grown water fleas wouldn't reproduce as fast in the waste water as they do in pure water. When the town officials hustled to Congress to find out why in the world the mating preferences of these amorous critters should be of any concern to water quality whatsoever, EPA officials were forced to drop their flea fine."[12]

Incredible, isn't it? All of this effectively points out that some of what goes on in the debate of the environment is so strange. There is a definite amount of hysteria out there.

References

1. *Citizen Outlook,* 11, (September/October 1996)

2. Alston Chase, "Bugs in environmentalism," from S.J. Milloy, www.junkscience.com (1997)

3. Ronald E. Gots, "Sick building syndrome industry grows," from S.J. Milloy, www.junkscience.com, (May 10, 1998)

4. Michael Fumento, "Sick of it all," *Reason,* 28 (2), (1996), 20

5. Stephen Barrett and Ronald E. Gots, *Chemical Sensitivity*, (Amherst, New York, Prometheus Books, 1998), 72

6. *The Energy Advocate*, 2, (March 1998)

7. *The DeWeese Report*, 2, (November 1996)

8. Peter Huber, *Hard Green*, (New York, Basic Books, 1999), 94

9. *Citizen Outlook*, 10, (November/December 1995)

10. Dixy Lee Ray, *Environmental Regulations: Costs & Benefits*, (Washington D.C., George C. Marshall Institute, March 1993), 14

11. R. Orford, "Alaska Allowed to Retain State Water Quality Standards for Arsenic," Alaska State Library Press Release #98-044, (February 23, 1998)

12. *Citizen Outlook*, 13, (October/November 1998)

Section 7:

The Lighter Side

Chapter 31

Chasing the Little White Ball

There are a thousand adages regarding golf, and those who do not golf (including myself) wonder why anyone would take up a game that seems to be more stressful than relaxing. I see no real fun in chasing a little white ball all over the place, no matter how pretty the walk (or drive) may be. But, golf is extremely popular here in the United States and golf courses are now opening at the rate of one per day, and have consumed more than a half million acres since 1987. As of 1998, they occupied about 3,800 square miles, an area three times the size of Rhode Island. There are now over 17,000 courses in the United States.[1]

Many environmental groups have recently been hammering golf courses as ecological disasters. According to Peter Gavin: "Environmentalists say golf courses, which average 250 acres for 18 holes, eat up valuable open space, sanitize wildlife habitat, require tons of pesticides annually and use 400,000 gallons of water per day (the average household consumes 325 gallons per day). Moreover, golf courses attract more development."[2]

With these questions in mind, let's take a look and see if all the fuss is true.

Concerns about water consumption, noise and air pollution from mowers, and chemicals used to marinate the soil, plus accounts of birds and fish being poisoned by pesticides have given environmentalists a poor opinion of the sport of golf. But people who design and operate golf courses have become increasingly conscious of the environment. "Integrated pest management," a philosophy that seeks to minimize chemical use, has become a way of life for golf course superintendents, as they have gained a better understanding of the risks some chemicals pose. Alex Markels quotes Sharon Newsome, environmental director for Physicians for Social Responsibility and formerly a National Wildlife Federation official who has scrutinized the golf industry since 1994: "There have been substantial environmental improvements over the past five years, particulary with new course construction."[1]

A 1995 meeting of golf industry leaders and environmentalists produced a document establishing voluntary environmental guidelines for new and existing courses. Subsequent meetings led to a pilot program to monitor fertilizer, pesticide, and water use at 50 courses across the country. Also, a golf course can now apply to be certified as an "Audubon Cooperative Sanctuary." Audubon International, a nonprofit organization not affiliated with the National Audubon Society monitors this program. The six-phase certification process entails a complete cataloging of plant and animal species, as well as a variety of steps to improve biodiversity and reduce pollution and waste. According to Audubon International: "Nearly 2,000 golf courses from around the world have joined this program, including more than 100 facilities in the U.S., eight in Canada and one in Spain receiving full certification by fulfilling requirements in all six categories."[3] Although this sounds great, those certified courses in the U.S. represent fewer than one percent of all courses in the U.S. Also, Ronald Dodson of Audubon International points out as many as half of all new golf course projects were not required to undergo a thorough environmental impact review.[1]

Golf courses often provide sanctuaries for various species of birds, thus attracting birdwatching clubs. For example, a study in Cincinnati showed conclusively that perching songbirds benefit from courses to the extent that they may be described as bird sanctuaries.[4] Carrying this a step further, a naturalized style of golf course design is conducive to wildlife management. James Beard and Robert Green report that typically, a course devotes 1.7 times more area to natural habitats such as roughs, woodlands, and water features than the combined area devoted to greens, tees, and fairways.[4] Courses also offer a way to reclaim landfills, mining operations, quarries, or other aesthetically or ecologically compromised sites. Here are some examples.

- The Old Works Golf Course was built on the once desolate site of a copper smelter near Anaconda, Montana. This had been declared a Superfund site because of arsenic pollution.[1] Designed by Jack Nicklaus, the course takes advantage of many remnants from the days the area was used to smelt copper.[5] Piles of black sand-like slag were used for all of the bunkers (sandtraps). Remnants of the smelter, such as massive stone furnace walls, line some of the fairways and fittingly, the course's 18th hole is called "Anode," for the smelter's final product, the copper anode bar. When the course opened in the spring of 1997, *Golf Magazine* called it the "most original new course of the decade."[5]

· The 120 acre Widow's Walk course occupies the site of an abandoned gravel mine near a garbage dump in Scituate, Massachussetts.[1]

· The Bay Harbor Golf Club in Bay Harbor, Michigan was built around an old limestone quarry and cement factory. This was a toxic waste site filled with 80 acres of kiln-dust piles that contained arsenic, lead, and other heavy metals.[1]

· The Coyote Hills Golf Course in Fullerton, California was built on a still-active Unocal oilfield. More than two million cubic yards of oil-drenched soils were treated for contamination and regraded. When biologists found newly endangered California gnatcatchers on the course, it was redesigned to preserve habitat for the songbirds.[1]

· The city of Santa Clara, California owned a landfill, half of which was capped in the 1970s and the other half in the 1980s. When a golf course was constructed on this land, the developers took steps to improve the site's environmental quality. Among other things, the golf course features a complex system of more than 100 wells to capture methane gas. Today, the course is home to a variety of wildlife, including waterfowl and other birds.[6]

The United States Golf Association (USGA) has contributed a great deal of money to lawn research and grass hybridization in the 20th century.[7] More than 80 percent of the lawns in the U.S. today contain grasses developed in the programs sponsored by the USGA since the 1960s. Since 1983, the USGA has funded more than 215 research projects at universities across the country at a cost of $21 million.[8] The program has three goals:

1. Develop turfgrasses for golf course that substantially reduce water use, pesticide applications, and maintenance costs.

2. Develop management practices for new and established turf that protect the environment while providing quality playing surfaces.

3. Determine the influence of golf and golf courses on the health and well being of individuals and communities.

Here are some of the projects the program sponsors:

- Researchers are studying turf at Purdue University's Kampen Golf Course to evaluate the natural ability of microbes to digest polluting chemicals in water runoff and turn them into harmless substances. This process, called bioremediation, could allow golf courses to be used as natural filters for waterborne pollution, such as antifreeze and road salt.[9]

- Purdue's researchers are also exploring the best way to plant new trees in areas where construction has removed old ones. Young, freshly planted trees don't do well in new developments because the topsoil has been stripped away and the remaining soil has been compacted by construction equipment. The researchers have planted some 1,300 trees on the Purdue golf course to study which planting methods work best.[10]

- At other golf courses, researchers are studying ways to better maintain native wildlife. One example is the Xerxes Society which is investigating how out-of-play areas can serve as habitats for pollinating bees and butterflies.[10] The Colorado Bird Observatory is studying golf courses and bird conservation and Audubon International has developed a data management system for information on wildlife habitat on golf courses.[9]

After doing all the research, I decided to visit a new facility (The Course Wente Vineyards in Livermore, California) to see what was going on. This Greg Norman-designed course opened in the summer of 1998, and I was curious to see how it was designed and is operated from an environmental standpoint. Jeff Shafer, Golf Course Superintendent, kindly provided this non-golfer with an extensive tour. I was impressed with the care management has shown the environment and with the beauty of the place. The course uses minimal fertilizer and limits the use of turfgrass or "rough," leaving many acres in a natural state. Wente averages less than four acres of turfgrass per hole, compared with the U.S. average of six to seven acres per hole.

The management also created a number of wetland sites, and they even minimize the spraying of trees. When I was there, workers were using high pressure air hoses to blow anthracnose-infected leaves to the ground rather than using chemical spray. Fertilizer is added via the watering sprinkling system as an intravenous drip might feed a hospital patient. This effectively minimizes the use of chemicals and eliminates the need to apply granular fertilizer. I was so taken with this place that it almost made me want to take up golf.

So, are all the questions answered? Probably not, but I can tell you this, as someone who has never played the sport, I can now at least understand why some folks want to chase a little white ball around beautiful terrain. It seems that the USGA and golf courses all across the U.S. are making strides toward being environmentally sound in their practices as well. Honestly, I think its just not as bad as some would have us believe.

References

1.   Alex Markels, "The Greening of America," *Audubon*, (July-August 1998), 42

2.   Peter Gavin, "Are golf courses really green?", *Palo Alto Weekly*, May 31, 1996

3.   Audubon Cooperative Sanctuary Program, www.usga.org/green/environment/audubon_program.html, accessed May 31, 2002

4.   James B. Beard and Robert L. Green, "The Role of Turfgrasses in Environmental Protection and Their Benefit to Humans," *Journal of Environmental Quality*," 23, (1994), 452

5.   Maria Streshinsky, "From Blighted to Beautiful," *VIA*, 120, (November/December 1999), 38

6.   *Golf and Wildlife*, (Far Hills, New Jersey, The USGA, 1994), 18

7.   Virginia S. Jenkins, *The Lawn: History of an American Obsession*, (Washington, Smithsonian Institution Press, 1994), 31

8.   "2001 Turfgrass and Environmental Research Summary," USGA, www.usga.org/green/research/reports/2001/index.html, accessed June 1, 2002

9.   *The USGA 1998 Turfgrass and Environmental Research Summary*, (Far Hills, New Jersey, The USGA, 1998)

10. "Golf Courses Become Living Laboratories," *The Futurist*, (March 1999), 7

Chapter 32

Noah — A Modern Version[1]

And the Lord spoke to Noah and said, "In six months I am going to make it rain until the whole Earth is covered with water and all of the evil people are destroyed, but I want to save a few good people and two of every living thing on the planet. I am ordering you to build an ark." And in a flash of lightning, he delivered the specifications for the ark. "Okay," Noah said, trembling in fear and fumbling with the blueprints.

Six months later it started to rain. Thundered the Lord, "You had better have my ark completed or learn to swim for a very long time," and six months passed. Rain continued to fall. The Lord saw that Noah was sitting in the front yard weeping.

"Noah," shouted the Lord, "where is my ark?" A lightning bolt crashed to the ground next to Noah. "Lord please forgive me," begged Noah. "I did my best but there were big problems."

"Regulations are flourishing. I am having a very difficult time learning all of them and new ones seem to appear daily. As an example, the 1998 *Federal Register's* 68,751 pages represent the highest count since the Carter presidency and a 6 percent jump over 1997.[2] Between April 1, 1996 and March 13, 2001 alone, federal regulatory agencies issued 21,653 final rules. Of those, 335 were defined as 'major' rules and those have an annual effect on the economy of more than $100 million each.[3]

"Here's one you might really appreciate Lord, since it's a follow-on of your ten commandments. A recent report titled *Ten Thousand Commandments*, tallies the price tag for implementing and sustaining federal regulations. The grand total is $688 billion per year."[4]

"Another example close to home is that of your Mother Theresa and her Missionaries of Charity, described by Philip Howard in his book titled *The Death of Common Sense*.[5] "Mother Theresa wanted to convert some abandoned buildings into homeless shelters in New York City, so the city offered the buildings at $1 each. The Missionaries of Charity set aside $500,000 for the reconstruction and the nuns developed a plan to provide temporary care for 64 homeless men in a communal setting. Although the city owned the buildings, no official had the authority to transfer them except through an extensive bureaucratic process. For a year and a half the nuns, only wanting to live a life of ascetic service, found themselves instead traveling in their sandals from hearing room to hearing room, presenting the details of the project and then discussing the details again at two higher levels of city government. In September 1989 the city finally approved the plan and the Missionaries of Charity began repairing the fire damage. However, after almost two years, they were told that New York's building code requires an elevator in every new or renovated multiple-story building. The Missionaries of Charity explained that because of their beliefs they would never use the elevator, which would also add upward of $100,000 to the cost. The nuns were told the law could not be waived even if an elevator didn't make sense. Mother Theresa gave up. She didn't want to devote that much extra money to something that wouldn't really help the poor."[5]

"Well, Mother Theresa's problems were minor compared to mine. First, I had to get a building permit for the ark's construction project, and your plans did not meet the code. So I had to hire an engineer to redraw the plans. Then I got into a big fight over whether or not the ark needed a fire sprinkler system."

My neighbors objected, claiming I was violating zoning by building the ark in my back yard. They were using the NIMBY principle, which means 'not in my back yard.' One book I read on this topic suggests that the way to handle this type of issue is to give the people something in return.[6] Could I offer them eternal happiness in Heaven, or perhaps at least free passage on the ark? Next, I had to get a variance from the City Planning Commission. Then I had a big problem getting enough wood for the ark because there was a ban on cutting trees because of the spotted owl. I had to convince the U.S. Fish and Wildlife Service that I needed wood to save the owl, but they would not let me catch any owls. Lastly, according to one report, each owl must have 7.7 million acres of habitat,[7] quite a bit more space than will be available on the ark. So that clinches it, no owls."

"It gets further complicated. Recently, for the first time, scientists have documented a case of an infection wiping out the last remnants of an entire species. The victim was a type of land snail that scientists were trying to pull back from the brink of extinction in a captive breeding program. This shows that captive breeding is not always a safe haven and one has to guard against infectious diseases when nursing species. The ark for all intents and purposes will be a captive breeding program – in other words, a form of zoo – and experts say that species need to be in the wild, not in zoos."[8]

"Next the carpenters formed a union and went on strike. I had to negotiate a settlement with the National Labor Relations Board before anyone could pick up a saw or hammer. Now I have 16 carpenters going on the boat and still no owl."

"I finally started gathering up animals and got sued by an animal rights group. They objected to me taking only two of each kind. Just when I got the lawsuit dismissed, the EPA notified me that I could not complete the ark without filing and environmental impact statement on the proposed flood. They did not take kindly to the idea that you had jurisdiction over your conduct and you were the supreme being."

"Then the Army Corps of Engineers wanted a map of the proposed flood plain. Right now I am still trying to resolve a complaint from the Equal Employment Opportunity Commission over how many minorities I am supposed to hire. Political science professor Aaron Wildavsky points out that after 30 years of expanding laws against workplace discrimination, Congress has succeeded in 'protecting' over 70 percent of all American workers. Many people, in fact, have multiple claims, and Wildavsky has calculated that if you apply all the protected categories, they add up to 374 percent of the American population."[9]

"Lastly, the IRS has seized all of my assets, claiming I am trying to avoid paying taxes by leaving the country. I just got a notice from the state about owing some kind of use tax. I really do not think I can finish your ark for at least another five years," Noah wailed.

Then the skies began to clear. The sun began to shine. A rainbow arched across the sky and Noah looked up with a smile. "You mean you are not going to destroy the Earth?" Noah asked hopefully.

"No," the Lord said sadly, "The government already has."

References

1. This originally appeared in *Environment and Climate News*, 3, (May 2000), 12. It was written by Rep. Gary Miller (R-California). I've taken the liberty to lengthen it in some spots and add a few references. Permission of the Heartland Institute to publish the original is greatly appreciated.

2. John Brignell, *Sorry Wrong Number*, (Great Britain, Brignell Associates, 2000), 218

3. "Earth Day 2002 Fact Sheet," The National Center for Public Policy Research," Washington, D.C., (April 15, 2002)

4. Dan Miller, "News from the Heartland," *Intellectual Ammunition*, 7, (November/December 1998), 2

5. Philip K. Howard, *The Death of Common Sense*, (New York, Warner Books, 1994), 3

6. Herbert Inhaber, *Slaying the Nimby Dragon*, (New Brunswick, New Jersey, Transactions Publishers, 1998)

7. William Dietrich, *The Final Forest*, (New York, Penguin Books, 1992), 191

8. Dan Ferber, "Bug Vanquishes Species," *Science*, 282, (October 9, 1998), 215

9. Philip K. Howard, *The Death of Common Sense*, 126

Index